Operations M
The Basics

THE BASICS OF BUSINESS SERIES

This series of books has been designed to cover the key functions of business at the fundamental level and is ideal for those who have no previous experience of business operations. These pocket-sized guides are descriptive and factual (but stop short of over-detailed analysis) and have been kept deliberately brief to make them accessible and inexpensive. Students taking business modules as part of courses in other disciplines, first year undergraduates seeking a foundation in business methods, and those undertaking HND and BTEC diplomas will find these sympathetically written books a perfect introduction to the world of business.

Forthcoming titles in this series:

Human Resource Management: The Basics
David Goss

Finance: The Basics
Peter Sneyd

Operations Management: The Basics

Les Galloway

Senior Lecturer, Department of Corporate Strategy
Leicester Business School, De Montfort University

Oxstalls Library
University of Gloucestershire
Oxstalls Campus, Oxstalls Lane
Longlevens, Gloucester
Gloucestershire
GL2 9HW

INTERNATIONAL THOMSON BUSINESS PRESS
I ⓣ P An International Thomson Publishing Company

London • Bonn • Boston • Johannesburg • Madrid • Melbourne • Mexico City • New York • Paris
Singapore • Tokyo • Toronto • Albany, NY • Belmont, CA • Cincinnati, OH • Detroit, MI

Operations Management: The Basics

Copyright ©1996 R.L. Galloway

First published by International Thomson Business Press

 A division of International Thomson Publishing Inc.
The ITP logo is a trademark under licence

British Library Cataloguing-in-Publication Data
A catalogue record for this book is available from the British Library

First edition 1996

Typeset in Times by Hodgson Williams Associates, Tunbridge Wells and Cambridge
Printed in the UK by Clays Ltd, St Ives plc, Bungay, Suffolk

ISBN 0-415-12568-5

International Thomson Business Press   International Thomson Business Press
Berkshire House   20 Park Plaza
168–173 High Holborn   14th Floor
London WC1V 7AA   Boston MA 02116
UK   USA

http://www.thomson.com/itbp.html

Contents

Figures

Preface

Operations is concerned with any productive activity, whether manufacturing or service, private or public sector, profit-making or not-for-profit. Operations management is concerned with ensuring that such activities are carried out both efficiently and effectively. Operations management is ubiquitous, and all of us are operations managers. Just getting up in the morning is an operation, and it requires a certain degree of management if it is to be achieved successfully. More importantly, every time we buy a product or undergo a service we are at the mercy of the design and management of the operation. The quality and value of the product or service are determined by the design and management of the operation that produced and supplied it.

From the point of view of the general public, an understanding of the operations function thus leads to a more informed consumer – someone in a better position to judge the likely quality and cost of the product or service and make a more informed decision.

From the point of view of the manager, all managers are operations managers and it is presumed that they are concerned that their departments should be efficient and effective, whatever their function. More importantly, operations is at the heart of all manufacturing and service enterprises, and unless the operations function is carried out effectively, there is little hope that the organisation as a whole will be effective. An understanding of operations management principles can thus not only help any manager manage more effectively, it can also contribute substantially to an understanding of the role and function of the organisation as a whole.

Operations is everyone's business, since ultimately effective and efficient operations lead to high-quality, high-value products and services.

This book has been written primarily as an introduction to the subject for those interested in the study of business and management in general. This will include students on courses of study where business is a peripheral issue, and those considering embarking upon a business or management course. The book is also aimed at anyone who, as an employee or a consumer, wishes to be better informed about the context of their work or their consumption.

Acknowledgements

Too many colleagues and students have contributed indirectly to this book for individual mention; however, I would in particular like to thank Bill Gage, who persuaded me that operations management was an important discipline when I first entered academe, and my colleague Bernard Colyer for fruitful discussion and comment on many aspects of this book. I would also like to thank my wife Carol and daughter Victoria for their encouragement and forbearance during its composition.

1 The nature and function of operations

INTRODUCTION

This chapter will set the agenda for the rest of the book, beginning with the definition of operations management. It will outline the structure of the book and discuss the importance of an awareness of operations management principles and practice. It will then go on to look at the role of operations management in manufacturing, service and not-for-profit organisations, and its relationship with the rest of the organisation.

DEFINITION

Historically, the term **operations management** has developed from a broadening of the concept of production management, which, as the name implies, was primarily concerned with the management of the conversion of raw materials into finished products for onward sale. As it became apparent that many of the techniques developed in production were equally applicable to administration and to the burgeoning service sector, the terminology was expanded to **production operations management, production and operations management, service operations** and finally just **operations management**.

The dictionary tells us that **operation** means:

> [the] way a thing works; piece of work; military activity; surgical work.

The common elements are activity and work, which in turn can be defined as purposeful activity, so the management of operations can be defined very simply as the management of work, or more precisely as the management of any productive activity. We are thus dealing with the management of production, or manufacturing, whereby physical material is transformed into finished product, for example raw potatoes into potato crisps, or electronic components into a television set. We are also dealing with the management of service industries, where more usually the state of the customer is transformed in some way. For example, a restaurant could be seen as transforming a hungry customer into a replete customer, or a bank, a financially disorganised customer into a person who is in financial control. (This does, of course, depend upon your view and experience of banks.) Operations management also applies to all the other activities which go to support the core activity of manufacturing the product or providing the service. These are also productive activities.

The meaning of management is frequently taken for granted, but it is worth defining here to avoid misunderstanding. Again the dictionary gives us a good starting point:

> to have control of; to operate effectively.

Operating effectively is usually taken to mean operating in a way which achieves the desired output. Management control is concerned with ensuring that this happens, but is also concerned with efficient use of resources, i.e. at lowest reasonable cost; thus operations management can be defined as:

> ensuring that productive activities are carried out effectively and efficiently.

STRUCTURE OF THE BOOK

Operations are transformations. Materials, components, information, customers, enter the process and are transformed, more or less successfully, by the resources of the process, into an output.

It might seem reasonable to start at the beginning and follow the process through to the end. This, however, presumes that the required end and the means of achieving it are well defined. This has rarely been the case in the past, and with rapidly developing technology and increasingly powerful consumers, it is even less likely now. Customer demands change rapidly. For an organisation to survive it must respond to, and even anticipate, these changes.

The starting point of a successful operation is the output, and no amount of efficiency in the transformation process will make up for an inappropriate design of product or service. For that reason, this book will follow a reverse order, looking first at the outputs – the design of the product or service – since failure to develop an appropriate design will result in little or no demand and render design of the operation irrelevant. The transformation process – the operation – will then be considered both from the point of view of its design and its management. Finally the inputs – materials and labour – will be considered.

WHY STUDY OPERATIONS?

Operations are ubiquitous. All commercial, governmental or charitable activities are concerned with using, usually limited, resources to achieve some sort of transformation. The case of manufacturing is obvious: raw materials are converted into a finished product whether it be raw beans and tomatoes into cans of baked beans, or complex mechanical and electronic components (themselves the output of other manufacturing processes) into a military aircraft.

In most service activities the transformation is also fairly obvious, and often the processes bear a strong resemblance to manufacturing. A hospital is expected to transform a sick client into a well client, but meanwhile the hospital kitchen is converting raw food into meals. The operation is perhaps less obvious in some governmental activities, partly because it is often very difficult to gain universal acceptance for clearly articulated objectives. Consideration of any social security system illustrates the possible conflict. Is its objective to ensure that no one suffers undue poverty and deprivation, or to ensure that the idle and feckless are made to make some effort to support themselves? A few moments' reflection suggests that it would be very difficult to design an efficient operation to achieve both of those objectives, but it would be a brave (and short-lived) politician who would wholeheartedly embrace either objective in a parliamentary democracy.

Where the nature of the transformation is clear, it is the task of operations management to ensure that it is carried out effectively and efficiently. A goal of good operations management is to ensure that the customer gets the best product or service, at the lowest cost. All customers are entitled to expect this. A knowledge of the context, techniques and constraints which apply to operations management can only increase our discrimination as customers, and therefore our power to influence the providers of products and services. An informed market can lead to better products and services at a more competitive cost, since it is more difficult to mislead or misdirect such a market, and a knowledge of operations assists in this. Of course, if a nation's manufacturers and service providers become more effective and efficient as a result of a discriminating home market, they become more competitive internationally and the national economy will therefore benefit.

A further benefit arises from the fact that we are all involved in an operations function in some way. If we are employed, we are, by definition, carrying out an operation. As we will see later, anyone using a service is, to a greater or lesser extent, also involved in an operation, and everybody uses services. A knowledge of operations management can be used to improve our own effectiveness and efficiency, both in our work and in our consumption of services. It could equally be used to improve efficiency in leisure activities, although this is not necessarily as desirable.

In summary, a knowledge of operations can on an individual scale:

- improve our purchasing power by increasing our awareness and discrimination;
- improve our personal effectiveness and efficiency in work and in using services.

And on a national scale it can:

- improve the competitiveness of manufacturing and service industries, and thus benefit the national economy.

THE ROLE OF OPERATIONS MANAGEMENT

Four distinct types of activity that may be described as operations have been identified.

- *Manufacturing* Physical materials are converted into a product which is then sold on to the customer. The customer may carry out further manufacturing operations, and the total chain, from extraction of raw materials to the supply of the product to the end consumer, may be quite long.

- *Supply* Where change of ownership of a physical good is the main activity. Retail distribution is the best-known example.

- *Transport* The movement of goods, or people, from one place to another without any physical change taking place.

- *Service* Changing the condition of the customer. This condition may be physical, as in dental surgery or hairdressing, intellectual, as in education, emotional, as in entertainment, or more often a complex mix of these and more.

It would be a mistake to consider these as distinct and separate categories. All manufacturers supply their end product to a customer, which will involve transporting the product, and there will be some element of service involved in handling enquiries and providing information. A convenient way of representing this overlap is through the operations tetrahedron, shown in Figure 1.1.

Any organisation will lie somewhere within the body of the tetrahedron, its position reflecting the relative importance it attaches to the four elements. No organisation lies at an apex of the tetrahedron – there is an element of service in every manufacture, supply or transport transaction, and no significant venture has been identified which can be classed as pure service.

The following examples illustrate the core operation of a number of organisations. All, of course, involve supply to some extent, but, unless otherwise specified, it is a relatively minor component.

- *Motor manufacturer* Mass market car manufacturers transform pre-manufactured components into cars. In some cases they also manufacture the components from raw materials, but more usually these are purchased from other manufacturers. They do not, as a rule, deal with the end customer, but supply the finished

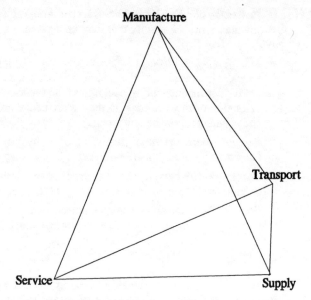

Figure 1.1 Operations tetrahedron (after Armistead and Kileya, 1984)

cars to dealers for onward selling, thus the supply and service elements of the business are small. While transport of goods to the customer is important, many organisations subcontract this role to a specialist. The transformation is thus primarily:

components $\Rightarrow$ finished product

and the operation is almost pure manufacture.

- *Restaurant (high-class)* The customer is buying an experience, probably a complex mixture of gastronomy, entertainment and image building. So the transformation is:

customer seeking satisfaction $\Rightarrow$ satisfied customer

Hunger is likely to be a small part of this satisfaction. While there are many manufacturing operations taking place behind the scenes (cooking food, cleaning dishes, linen etc.) the main operation is service.

- *Restaurant (self-service)* The customer is buying a meal, so the transformation is:

    hungry customer ⇒ satisfied customer

    but most of the operations effort will be devoted to food preparation:

    raw materials ⇒ prepared meals

    The focus of the operation lies somewhere between manufacture, service and supply.

- *Self-service supermarket* The presumption behind all self-service operations is that the customer knows what they want. Such shops do not provide advice or assistance to any great extent. The transformation is:

    customer with identified needs ⇒ satisfied customer

    The focus of the operation is supply, with a limited amount of service.

- *Specialist food retailer* Unlike the self-service supermarket, here the customer would expect to be able to discuss requirements with a knowledgeable assistant and obtain advice. The transformation process is essentially the same, except that the needs do not need to be as clearly identified, but the operation is now supply with a substantial amount of service. Supply is still dominant: without the goods to sell, the advice becomes irrelevant.

- *Insurance company* Insurance companies generally maintain that they are selling investment and protection. In fact, insurance does not protect against the occurrence of the insured event, but provides for financial compensation if the event occurs, so protection is perhaps an overstatement. An investment model of the transformation might be:

    customer with some money
    ⇒ customer with more money

    In the case of protection, the truly satisfied customer is the one for which nothing happens, but since that is outside the control of the company, an alternative is:

> customer suffering a loss
> $\Rightarrow$ customer financially compensated for the loss

Both of these transformations are too long-term to be used as a basis for managing the operation, and shorter-term transformations of the type:

> customer seeking financial advice
> $\Rightarrow$ properly advised customer

and:

> customer seeking compensation $\Rightarrow$ compensated customer

define the operation as almost pure service.

- *Criminal court* Once one moves away from profit-making organisations to social, governmental and charitable organisations, problems can arise in identifying the customer. A criminal court is obviously a service, since it does not manufacture, transport or supply. The question is 'Who is the beneficiary?' The alternatives in this case are:
  — the accused; this hardly makes sense, unless the accused is wrongly acquitted, but that would represent a quality failure;
  — the legal profession; they certainly benefit financially, but that cannot seriously be considered to be the main function of the operation;
  — government; a cynical view might be that since most of the electorate abhor crime, governments must be seen to be tackling crime, and the court is a manifestation of this. The key transformation becomes:

> government $\Rightarrow$ more popular government

You must decide for yourself whether this reflects your view;
  — society; the general consensus is that crime is undesirable, and the criminal court is one aspect of the control of crime. The transformation is:

> society troubled by crime $\Rightarrow$ society with less crime

The service is thus to society, but the actual operation which leads to this is:

> apprehended criminal $\Rightarrow$ imprisoned criminal

The criminal may well be a person, but the most suitable model is probably the manufacturing model, with the criminal as the material being processed.

These examples illustrate the fact that the ease of definition of the operation varies considerably. It is relatively easy where goods are involved, it is more difficult with services, and more difficult still in not-for-profit activities. In the latter case, personal viewpoint also plays a part. You might legitimately take the view that the criminal justice system exists as much to protect the innocent as to punish or deter the guilty. This viewpoint might well be modified, however, if you return home to find that your house has been burgled.

It is important to consider the nature of the operation carefully, to look at and explicitly reject alternatives, rather than assume the obvious, if the enterprise is to be successful. An insurance company with a very effective and efficient investment operation, but a poor customer contact operation, will not do as well as a company with an effective and efficient customer contact operation, but a mediocre investment operation. The former company may be best in terms of the core operation of:

customer with some money $\Rightarrow$ customer with more money

but the latter will attract and convert more customers because it is better at:

customer seeking financial advice $\Rightarrow$ properly advised customer

The successful organisation considers all aspects of its operation.

For operations management to be successful, the function of the operation must first be defined. The degree to which this is achieved is a measure of effectiveness, the key objective of operations management. Efficiency is less important since there is no point in carrying out an irrelevant, or worse damaging, activity efficiently. Effectiveness means achieving objectives, efficiency means consuming minimum resources. While both are desirable, the former is of overriding importance.

In commercial organisations, increasing effectiveness leads to increasing sales and thus greater revenue. Increasing efficiency leads to reducing costs. Since

$$\text{profit} = \text{revenue} - \text{cost}$$

both together increase profit. Good operations management gives a twofold enhancement to profitability.

The case in not-for-profit organisations is less clear. The difficulty arises mainly because of the separation of the roles of user and paymaster. Where an agency is funded by central government, or by charitable donations, then there is a tendency for it to operate in a manner acceptable to its paymasters rather than the users. If this proves ineffective as far as the users are concerned, their ability to influence the operation is limited. The influence of voters on politicians with regard to issues of detail is not great; the influence of the recipients of charity is even less. As we have seen, a clear public statement of objectives is also unlikely. The net result of this is that lack of coordination, caused by individual managers following their own perceptions of what the organisation is about, is more likely to arise in such organisations. (There are, of course, private sector organisations which show exactly this behaviour, and not-for-profit organisations which have well-established and coherent objectives – the differences are a matter of degree.) In the absence of clear objectives, operations management tends to assume that what is being done is sensible and seeks to carry it out efficiently.

Even efficiency is not necessarily seen as an unalloyed good in not-for-profit organisations. In an ideal world a public health authority or a hospital with a fixed budget should be able to increase the amount of treatment it gives (its effectiveness) within that budget by exercising greater efficiency. In practice, the result of greater efficiency is often simply a reduced budget which, while it might be in the interests of the community as a whole, is of no benefit to the hospital.

Good operations management is desirable in the private sector because it has a direct effect on profit. Its less obvious desirability in the public and not-for-profit sectors is mainly due to a failure of political will and inadequate definition of objectives and priorities, rather than to any intrinsic shortcomings in operations management.

RELATIONSHIP WITH THE REST OF THE ORGANISATION

A traditional functional division of a manufacturing organisation is shown in Figure 1.2. While detailed structure is highly varied, the variations are minor compared with the commonality. Operations is at the heart of the organisation, since without it the other functions would be superfluous. This is not to say that it is indispensable. Many organisations completely subcontract the manufacturing function.

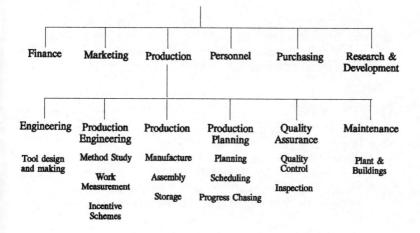

Figure 1.2   Functional division in manufacturing

More recently, the impact of business process re-engineering has led to a growing interest in non-functional structures directed towards customer needs rather than internal needs. This trend moves the organisation towards a service structure, where the operations function is more dispersed and may not even be named.

In this case a better view is that operations is ubiquitous. All tasks and functions are operations and should be viewed as means of achieving organisational objectives efficiently.

SUMMARY

Operations has been defined as any productive activity, and thus as a transformation process. It is implicit in the definition that this transformation adds value, otherwise the outcome would not be saleable.

Operations management is defined as managing the process of transformation to maximise both efficiency and effectiveness. As we will see later in the book, effectiveness is sometimes neglected in the pursuit of efficiency.

A number of examples of the transformation process have been discussed in order to illustrate the importance of appropriate definition, and the role of operations mangement in manufacturing and non-manufacturing organisations. The operations tetrahedron has been introduced as a useful way of classifying operations.

Finally the relationship between operations management and other parts of the organisation has been described.

QUESTIONS

In your own organisation, what is the core transformation? Does the organisation behave as if it were the core activity?

Where does your organisation fit within the Operations Tetrahedron?

Does the organisational perception match the customer expectation? Be critically aware of the transformation that you appear to be being subjected to when undergoing a service.

REFERENCE

Armistead C G & Killeya J C (1984) 'Transfer of concepts between manufacture and service', *International Journal of Operations and Production Management*, 3 (3)

FURTHER READING

The transformation process model of operations, while it predates systems thinking, is very well captured by that approach. Those wishing to pursue it further might start with:

Patching, D. (1990) *Practical Soft Systems Analysis*, Pitman

There are numerous more detailed books on Operations Management. Two which are worth starting with are:

Galloway, R. L. (1993) *Principles of Operations Management*, Routledge

Slack, Chambers, Harland, Harrison, Johnston, (1995) *Operations Management*, Pitman

2 Outputs

INTRODUCTION

There has been a great deal of discussion as to whether, from an operations viewpoint, there is any significant difference between a product and a service. Products, after all, are provided and sold to customers, as are services.

A product can be defined as a physical good which is manufactured then sold to a customer to do with as the customer sees fit. The customer is not involved in the process of production at all, and the interaction between the customer and the producer is minimal. The process is represented diagrammatically in Figure 2.1.

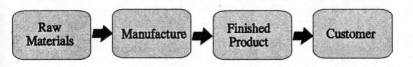

Figure 2.1 A model of manufacturing

The American Marketing Association defines a service as 'Activities, benefits or satisfaction which are offered for sale or provided in connection with the sale of goods.' A service thus generally involves the customer undergoing a process which is, presumably, of benefit or value to that customer. This might involve

15

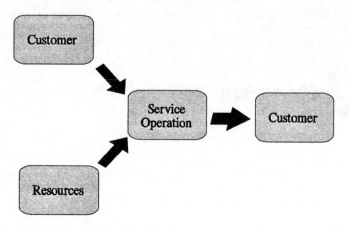

Figure 2.2   A model of service

physical change to the customer, as in a cosmetic or medical service, mental change, as in entertainment, a change in the level of knowledge, as in education or advice services, or even a change in state of physical possessions, as in retail sales. This is represented diagrammatically in Figure 2.2.

As was discussed in Chapter 1, product and service are not in fact different in essence, but are merely the opposite extremes of a spectrum. Any transaction between a supplier and a customer involves interaction, i.e. processing of the customer. The essential difference between product and service is that the customer is not involved in the production of a product, but is heavily involved in the production of a service. All the other differences stem from this. However, since products must eventually be sold, and this involves the customer, there is an element of service in all operations.

PRODUCTS

Products are physical objects which are produced for sale, or to contribute to the production of other products or services. For example, in the manufacture of surf boards, the mould shop will manufacture the moulds which are used to cast the boards from glass reinforced plastic. The moulds are certainly products; however, they are not intended for resale, but to facilitate the manufacturing process.

The actual chain of manufacture may be quite long and involve a number of different organisations. Figure 2.3 shows part of the route involved in manufacturing a simple portable radio. It is illustrative only, but shows that five or more different organisations

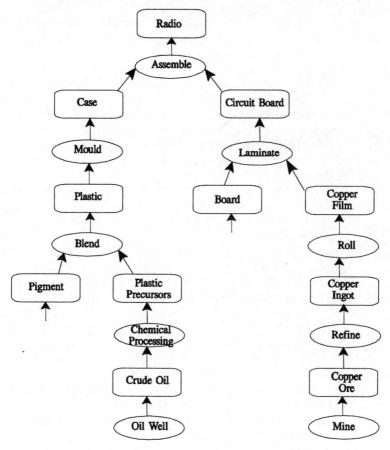

Figure 2.3 Partial map of manufacture of radio

can be involved in the chain providing only one component of the finished product. One characteristic of this is that stock may be held at virtually any point in the process. The refiner of copper is not refining it to order, but is maintaining significant stocks, in part because the cost of starting and stopping the refining process is likely to be greater than the cost of operating it continuously.

Since products have a well-defined physical existence, their characteristics can be specified. A product specification may be functional – for example, a washing powder's specification might be that it should remove grease from cotton on a standard washing cycle at 40°C. Or a specification may be physical – for example, a 24 mm number 6 wood screw should be 24 mm ±1 mm in length.

Physical characteristics are obviously easier to measure and control, so they are usually preferred. In the example of the washing powder, manufacturing would work to a physical specification giving the relative quantities of the various ingredients of the powder. Research and development would have identified this mix as achieving the desired results, and quality assurance would periodically test the output to ensure that it continued to function as specified.

The ability to specify the physical characteristics of a product in measurable terms (physical characteristics includes not only size, but density, strength, colour, texture, electrical characteristics, etc.) means that, at least in theory, it is possible for manufacturer and customer to reach a complete and unambiguous agreement on the product specification. This frequently happens in industrial supply. The manufacturer of the ICs used by the portable radio assembler will be working to a comprehensive specification. However, there is usually scope for misunderstanding.

When products were simple and demand exceeded capacity, service was of little relevance to manufacturing operations. As supply has expanded and products have become more and more sophisticated, so competition has intensified, and the areas where this has been most obvious have been quality, flexibility and service. Quality will be considered later in the chapter. Flexibility – the ability of a manufacturer to respond to rapid changes in customer or market requirements – has been addressed by manufacturing organisations becoming leaner and more agile. It is also an aspect of service – the

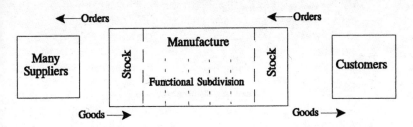

Figure 2.4   Historic operations context

ability to anticipate and respond to customer needs. Products are now obsolete, except as a means to satisfy customer needs, and increasingly, world class manufacturing organisations are recasting themselves as service organisations, whose mission is to anticipate and satisfy customer needs. No longer is it a matter of selling products, but of solving problems. The aim is to become the preferred supplier and establish a degree of partnership, thus excluding the competition.

The historic operations context of manufacturing is shown in Figure 2.4.

Here, the manufacturing operation was isolated as much as possible from both suppliers and customers. This allowed products to be manufactured as efficiently as possible, without interference from customers or suppliers. Stocks of both raw materials and finished products were held to isolate production from the unreliability of suppliers and the unpredictability of the market. Customers were either supplied from stock, or had to wait, while suppliers were simply not trusted. As many sources of supply as possible were established and they were played off against each other to achieve the best price.

While efficient, this was a low-service, low-flexibility type of operation. The lack of flexibility was especially great, since any change in output would require that all existing stocks be worked through first.

The developing picture is shown in Figure 2.5.

Here, the pressure for customer service and responsiveness means that close communication must be maintained with the

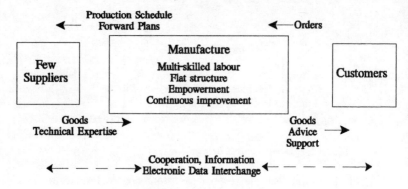

Figure 2.5 Emerging operations context

customer. This is achieved by means of electronic data interchange (EDI) between supplier and customer computers, but also frequently by having individuals or teams permanently resident on customers' premises. This focus on collaborative problem-solving rather than product supply implies quite different organisational structures, focused externally upon the customer. This is achieved by adopting **business process re-engineering** (BPR), a reincarnation of the 1970s systems design methodologies, which rejects existing structures and redesigns the organisation to meet its prime objective of customer satisfaction.

In order to preserve flexibility, stocks are eliminated through the use of just-in-time (JIT) methods. This requires close co-operation with suppliers, so it becomes necessary to have fewer suppliers, and to cultivate and trust them. Again, EDI facilitates communication. Having reached this point, it makes sense to use suppliers' design expertise; **simultaneous engineering** involves suppliers being given design specifications for new products and asked to design the components that they will supply.

Two examples of this blurring of boundaries will suffice.

- A manufacturer of heavy industrial equipment no longer purchases fastenings (nuts, bolts, clips, etc. used to fasten components together). Instead, a specialist fastenings supplier maintains appropriate stocks of fastenings on the shop floor under contract. Decisions on stock levels, sourcing, delivery and even the physical maintenance of the storage areas are all subcontracted.

- A garment design brand is sold through a network of retail franchises. All outlets have point of sale terminals that are connected, using EDI, to central computers. These computers continuously monitor trends in sales and automatically arrange for despatch of consignments to the outlets and for replenishment of stocks from manufacturers. To facilitate flexibility, many garments are stocked finished except for final dyeing, so that this can be fine-tuned to match the demand of the market for different colours.

What these examples illustrate is the growing importance of service in what have traditionally been non-service activities. The products must still be made, but this is no longer enough. A further consequence of this, in many cases, is the blurring of the boundaries between customer and supplier. Just as the responsive manufacturing organisation is one where the structure is directed towards satisfying customers rather than maintaining discrete functions, so the structural divisions in the chain of supply are blurring in response to the quest by the final company in the chain to excel in satisfying the final customer.

SERVICE

A substantial element of any service is likely to be intangible. The involvement of physical, i.e. tangible, objects in service is limited, and frequently peripheral. The food at a restaurant is tangible and important, but the ambience and service may be more important in determining customers' satisfaction. The fact that people can become 'merry' on soft drinks at a party if the atmosphere is convivial enough demonstrates the dominance of the intangible (atmosphere) over the tangible (alcohol). The customer is undergoing a process, and the meaning of that process to the customer is internal to the customer. Most of the characteristics, and characteristic difficulties, of a service stem from customer involvement. Widely accepted differences which set services apart are as follows.

- *The customer is part of the service process* The service cannot take place in the absence of the customer, even if many of the more tangible components may be processed in anticipation, or out of sight, of the customer. The customer at a restaurant may not be involved in the preparation of the meal, and certainly will not be involved in the purchasing of the raw materials, but must be present during the serving of the meal for the service to exist at all.

- *Production and consumption of the service are simultaneous* This is an inevitable outcome of the necessary presence of the customer.

- *Service cannot be stocked* The manufacture and final use of products may be separated by weeks, or even years. Even some processed foods have shelf lives of several years. The simultaneous production and consumption of services, however, means that stock cannot exist. Stock is something that can be retained for future use, and must not be confused with surplus capacity that, if unused, is wasted. This is sometimes described as volatility.

- *Service demand is extremely variable* Demand variability is an important issue in both manufacturing and services, but while manufacturing is concerned about demand variation over a year or more, services often show large demand variation from hour to hour. Figure 2.6 shows the likely demand pattern for urban public transport over a week.

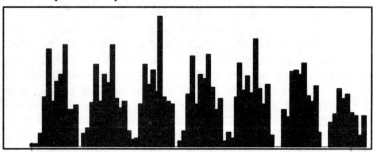

Time

Figure 2.6 Relative demand for public transport over one week

- *The perception of the service is subjective* To a degree customers' perception of a service will depend upon their expectations and experience. There is unlikely to be an agreed specification covering all aspects of a service; indeed, given the variety of customers, such a specification would be impossible. For example, a careful explanation of some aspect of the service might be seen as helpful and informative by one customer, but patronising by another. What is friendly service to one person, might be seen as obsequious by another, and over-familiar by a third. Service involves interpersonal interaction, which is notoriously difficult to standardise and control, but even something as measurable as waiting time can give rise to quite different perceptions.

All of these differences between manufacture and service are, of course, a matter of degree, and with the increasing stress on service in world class manufacturing organisations, the distinction is becoming less obvious.

It can be said that where a world class manufacturer is striving to provide an excellent product (tangible) backed up by an excellent service, the world class service-provider is seeking to provide an excellent service backed up by excellent tangibles.

The differences are, nevertheless, still very real, and of great significance to operations. There are potentially as many services as there are customers. This, together with the intangibility, makes specification and design a problem of much greater magnitude in services. The service-providing operation is the service, whereas the manufacturing operation is not the product. While it may not necessarily be sensible, it is possible to design a product, then to select a manufacturing method, a separation that is impossible in service design. Matching supply and demand is much more difficult with services, because demand is much more variable and stock is not available. Manufacturing operations frequently use stock to buffer supply and demand. The intangibility of services and the subjectivity of service customers makes the definition, measurement and control of quality especially difficult. It is perhaps ironic that an area which is seen by many as the main field for competition – service quality – is not at present subject to any agreed definition or measurement.

QUALITY

Quality is perhaps the most difficult concept of all in the field of operations. Everyone assumes that they know what it is, but it is in fact a very elusive concept. Dictionaries usually refer to a degree of excellence, but this ignores the concept of value, and a good quality product or service may well be one that is affordable, rather than one that is excellent.

Three types of quality can be distinguished, and it is a failure to discriminate between them that leads to much of the confusion. These are:

- *Design quality* The degree to which the specification of the product or service meets the needs of the market. This is often described as **fitness for purpose**.

- *Conformance quality* The degree to which the operations system provides products or services that meet specification.

- *Operational quality* The degree to which the process produces products or services that meet specification without failure. The **total quality** approach represents one extreme of this in the term 'right first time'.

Ideally, in industrial markets, design quality is well-specified, and there is agreement between supplier and customer on the specification of the product. In practice, however, specifications are rarely so comprehensive and unambiguous that misunderstandings cannot arise. It is usually accepted that there is a trade-off between cost and specification, and 'good' quality thus becomes a balance between specification and price.

In consumer goods this trade-off is still implicit, but the customer has neither the opportunity, nor the technical competence, to negotiate specification. There is therefore scope for disappointment and perceived poor quality, even when the goods meet specification.

The problem with services is further compounded by the subjectivity and intangibility of much of the service transaction. This is discussed further in Chapter 4.

It can be argued that the operations responsibility lies with conformance quality and operational quality. Once the product/service is designed and the operation has been set up, this is true, but an operations input into product design helps ensure that the product specification is realistic, while the design of a service is synonymous with the design of the service operation.

SUMMARY

The outputs of the operation have traditionally been perceived as *either* products *or* services. Products are physical goods which conform to laid-down specifications. They are more or less permanent, and they are usually created in the absence of the customer. They are predictable and tangible.

Services are characterised by the transformation, to a greater or lesser extent, of the customer. Of necessity, they are therefore produced in the presence of the customer and with the customer's participation. This gives rise to a range of characteristics such as volatility, variability and intangibility that are not present in production operations and which conspire to complicate the operations task.

Recent trends are blurring the distinction between product and service, as manufacturers strive to achieve competitive advantage by adding value to their products and establishing co-operative relationships.

The perception that buyers of goods actually require a service is not new, although it has only recently been embraced wholeheartedly:

> The emphasis...is upon the services of goods, not upon the goods themselves. Goods are wanted because they are capable of performing services – favourable events which occur at a point in time. (Morris, 1941)

Quality of output has always been a key issue in determining competitiveness, but increasing global competition has again served to raise its profile. Quality can be a vague and slippery concept, but three alternative types of quality have been defined in an attempt to clarify this.

QUESTIONS

Considering the organisation you thought of in Chapter 1, to what extent is it providing a product or a service?

How important is the relative balance between these to its customers? Does the organisation recognise that balance?

When you purchase a service, consider the relative balance of product and service in the transaction, and their relative importance to you. Would a change on the part of the service-provider increase or reduce the likelihood that you would continue using the service?

REFERENCE

Morris, R.T. (1941) *The Theory of Consumer's Demand*, Yale University Press

FURTHER READING

An excellent overview of the service concept is found in:

Normann, R. (1991) *Service Management*, John Wiley.

For an exploration of the 'servicisation' of manufacturing, see:

Vandermerwe, S. (1993) *From Tin Soldiers to Russian Dolls*.

3 Product design

Entia non sunt multiplicanda praeter necessitatum.

William of Ockham (c. 1300)

KISS (Keep it simple, stupid).

Anonymous paraphrase (modern)

INTRODUCTION

Product design itself is not strictly a direct concern of operations; however, operations has to live with the output of the design process. If the designed product is difficult to make, unreliable, incompatible with existing processes, then at best manufacture is going to be inefficient, at worst it will fail completely and damage the manufacture of existing successful products.

This chapter will give an overview of the sources of design pressure, and some of the approaches to design. Most of the issues discussed are also relevant to service design.

SOURCES OF DESIGN PRESSURE

New design arises in response to three possible pressures:

- *Market pull* Demand arises for a new, or changed, product from the market place. Rapidly changing consumer expectations are the prime generator of this pressure.

27

- *Technology push* Technological advance results in the possibility of producing a hitherto impossible product. Of course if one company introduces such a product, and it is successful, this is a source of market pull for other potential suppliers.

- *Re-equipment* The need to replace obsolete or worn out process plant gives rise to an opportunity to redesign products.

Market pull and technology push are frequently intertwined, but the demand for notebook computers, for instance, is an example of a market driving technology. The increasing reliance of the executive on IT facilities meant that the travelling executive, of whom there are many, needed a portable computing facility to function effectively. Whether there is a real need, except in status terms, for the £5,000 all-singing, all-dancing notebook computer is less certain.

A successful example of technology push is the development of electronic point-of-sale terminals. Originally electro-mechanical cash registers were considered perfectly satisfactory, but purely electronic cash registers became available more cheaply and more reliably as electronic technology developed in the 1960s and 1970s. The transition from the electronic cash register to the point of sale terminal was probably mainly the result of market pull.

A rather less successful innovation is the wrist-watch calculator. This is an example of miniaturisation for its own sake, but lacking functionality because of the difficulties of using and reading something so small.

Once a development begins, an endless cycle of market pull–technology push often follows. When desktop computing became established as a market, a cycle of software designers producing ever more sophisticated packages, either in response to perceived need, or to achieve differentiation in the market, caused continuous pressure on hardware manufacturers to produce ever more powerful and compact machines. Figure 3.1 contrasts the hardware of the early 1980s with that of the mid-1990s.

This shows the very rapid development in power, with a substantial reduction in real cost.

Figure 3.1 Typical PC Configurations

	Early 1980s	*Mid-1990s*
CPU	8 bit 8 Mhertz	32 bit 66 Mhertz
RAM	128 kilobytes	8 megabytes
Display	20cm monochrome	35cm high-resolution colour
Storage	360 kilobyte floppy disc	500 megabyte hard disc 1.44 megabyte floppy disc 600 megabyte CD-ROM drive

Whatever the origin of the initiative, a design process will usually begin with market research, intended to establish both the characteristics of the product required, and of the market requiring it. Physical appearance, function, size and durability are obvious product issues, but price, volume of likely demand and the variability of both demand and design are also essential for effective manufacture. Obvious though this may seem, market research is not always carried out and designs or design changes are introduced on the basis of capability, or even just a hunch. Consequently they usually fail, although when successful they do have the merit of being faster to market, with a lower risk of the competition gaining early knowledge of the development.

SIMULTANEOUS ENGINEERING

While lack of market research is, fortunately, rare, lack of consultation with operations is still all too common. Operations is presented with a product design and expected to get on and make it. Provided that the new product lies well within the existing range of products and processes, this should not be a problem, but once significant deviation occurs, the results can be catastrophic. Indeed deviations need not be so great, as the following cases show.

- A major savoury snack manufacturer redesigned its product range, changing from waxed paper to foil bags. All seemed well until retailers began to complain in large numbers about burst bags. The new foil bags were not as compressible as the old paper bags. As a result, far more force was needed to seal the cardboard cartons in which they were shipped, resulting in substantial numbers of bags bursting. Neither larger cardboard cartons, nor fewer bags per carton were desirable alternatives.

- A manufacturer of cardboard cartons won a contract from a cigarette manufacturer. Because cigarettes are prone to forgery (local bootleg manufacturers package low-grade products to look like imported prestige brands), even the outer packing cases were required to be made to a very tight tolerance. This message did not get through to operations. As a result the first major consignment was rejected by the customer for failing to meet quality standards, even though it was of the standard supplied by the manufacturer to other customers.

In both of the above cases problems arose because operations had not been consulted, or not to a sufficient degree, before the product design was implemented.

One effect of increasing competition and globalisation of markets has been an increase in pressure to get to market quickly. The increasing pace of technological development only increases this need. A firm that is slow to market with a new product will find at best that the competition catches up very quickly, and at worst that the competition is already there. Indeed, the product may already have been superseded. Success is now critically dependent upon time to market, and the shorter this is, the longer the period during which reasonable profits can be gained, and, of course, profit is essential to fund new development.

These pressures have led directly to the concept of **simultaneous engineering**. This was originally conceived as a means of shortening time to market, and increasing reliability, by involving manufacturing at an early stage in the design process. This has a two-way benefit. Manufacturing can advise design on those areas where they have strengths, so that the design can build upon these. Equally, manufacturing are aware as early as possible of the need for new plant and methods. When the product design comes to manufacture, manufacture is ready for it. Prior to simultaneous engineering, it was not unusual for design and manufacturing to communicate only for the purpose of exchanging recriminations. Products were late to market because manufacturing did not start preparations until the design stage was finished, and they were unreliable because the product was not necessarily suitable for the manufacturing skills and technology used.

The increasing tendency to co-operation along the supply chain has led to simultaneous engineering being extended to include suppliers. Instead of waiting until a detailed product design has been completed and then seeking suppliers of fully specified components, suppliers are presented with functional designs at an early stage, and expected to use their own design skills to produce the required components. The effect of these developments on time scale is shown in Figure 3.2.

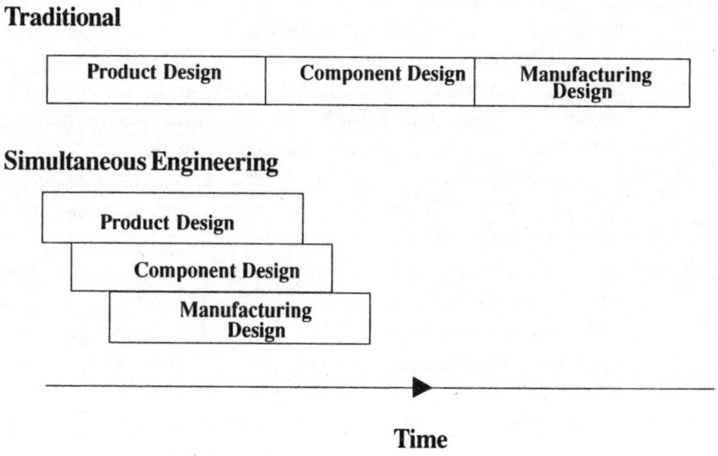

Traditional

Product Design	Component Design	Manufacturing Design

Simultaneous Engineering

Product Design

Component Design

Manufacturing Design

Time

Figure 3.2 Effect of simultaneous engineering on time to market

This approach is not without its dangers. Production may equip itself for a product whose design fails; suppliers risk an investment in product development which might not be successful; releasing details of new product intentions to suppliers increases the risk of knowledge reaching the competition. However, on balance the advantages seem to outweigh the disadvantages.

DESIGN FOR MANUFACTURE

Design for manufacture and design for reliability go hand in hand. A product that is easy to make, lies well within the manufacturing process capabilities and uses methods familiar to both management and labour will be made consistently and well. One that uses unfamiliar technology, is more demanding of precision in its assembly, or is complex to assemble, is more likely to fail either during or after manufacture. The general advice, therefore, is always to design within process capabilities. This is, of course, impossible. If it were adopted as standard practice, we would still be using flint tools. Some organisations are always willing to lead the way into uncharted technologies, and the rewards can be considerable (Apple Computers and Microsoft Corporation are examples of success) but the risks are also great (Sinclair Electronics, for example). The demand for high-speed, high-resolution colour screens for laptop computers is such that very unreliable production technology is economically viable. Some three years after their introduction, 70 per cent of production was still being scrapped, hence the £500+ premium on the price of machines with this technology.

Reliability of manufacture and reliability of the final product is linked directly to the number of processes involved in manufacture, and the number of components in the product. If a single component has a failure rate of, say, 1 per cent, then two such components linked together in the same product will give a failure rate of 1.9 per cent, and ten a failure rate of 9.6 per cent. For the mathematically minded, the equation is:

Failure rate for n components $= 100(1 - (1-f/100)^n)$

where f is the percentage failure rate of one component.

Exactly the same effect arises with the number of process stages in manufacture, where f is now the failure rate of each process. Figure 3.3 shows the effect graphically.

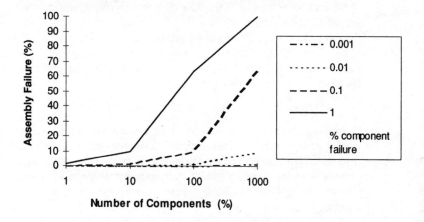

Figure 3.3 Product and component failure

Modern electronic and mechanical products are enormously complicated, hence the demands for high-quality components. Without integrated circuits, modern electronics could not exist – not because of the cost of using discrete components, though this would be prohibitive, but simply because they could not be made to function reliably enough. The eight or so memory chips in a personal computer replace the equivalent of 100,000,000 or more individual transistors and associated components. Even with an individual component failure rate as low as 1 in 100,000,000, the overall failure rate of the product would be about 62 per cent. A component reliability less than this would make successful manufacture impossible.

VALUE ANALYSIS
Value analysis, and the closely related **value engineering**, are

approaches to product design that are aimed at simplifying the product without diminishing its attractiveness in the market place.

Value analysis begins by identifying the function(s) of the product. This is followed by a detailed analysis of the design and construction of the product, with a view to eliminating any elements that do not contribute to function.

It is important that all the functions that a product serves are identified, and generally these should be linked to price. Value analysis identifies two elements which together give the value of the product:

exchange value = useful value + esteem value.

Exchange value is a measure of what the market is prepared to pay for the product, while useful value is a measure of how valuable the main function of the product is. Esteem value attempts to assign a value to attributes of the product that do not directly contribute to its usefulness, but nevertheless make it attractive to the market.

As an example, a reliable second-hand 2CV car, costing about £3,000, fulfils all the required functions of travelling to work in an urban area. Despite this, many people use cars costing £15,000 or more almost exclusively for this purpose. Value analysis suggests that the esteem value of such a car must therefore be £12,000.

In order to ensure that esteem issues are not missed, and that function is not compromised, value analysis is always a team task. Since a large team is unwieldy, a core team of five or six members who can call on others when required is preferred. It is usual to target complex multi-component products, as these yield more potential for saving than products consisting of very few components.

Value analysis is usually carried out following Gage's twelve steps:

1. *Select the product* Complex products give the greatest potential for individual improvement, but those with a large usage can give a large total potential saving. Long-established products give a higher chance that technical development will have increased the potential for improvement. If no product falls

into any of these categories, then value analysis may not be recommended.

2. *Extract the cost* An accurate marginal cost is required, since this is what value analysis seeks to reduce. Overheads are not included.
3. *Record the components.*
4. *Record all the functions* This involves the whole team, and usually brainstorming is used to overcome prior assumptions. The object is to identify the functions which the customer may be looking for, not the functions which the manufacturer thinks are appropriate.
5. *Record present and future demand.*
6. *Determine the primary function* This involves eliminating functions identified in step 4 which can be classed as secondary, until only one function is left.
7. *List other ways of achieving the primary function* Again a whole team activity involving brainstorming.
8. *Cost the alternatives* This is done as soon as possible after brainstorming, but not during brainstorming, since it would then inhibit the generation of ideas.
9. *Investigate the three cheapest alternatives* Three is an arbitrary cut-off, but is usually found to be adequate. Detailed study of feasibility, performance and cost is carried out.
10. *Choose the best alternative.*
11. *Identify the additional functions which need to be incorporated* Functions identified at step 4 and not already incorporated by step 10 can now be introduced if required. If necessary, further work to produce a detailed design is carried out.
12. *Ensure acceptance* Inertia and vested interests can be substantial obstacles to successful implementation. The value analysis team must be prepared to sell their proposal within the organisation, and a strong case including detailed costing and cost savings, implementation plans and models or prototypes will be required.

Value analysis is a widely used cost-reduction technique; however, some designers maintain that it should not be used at all since it

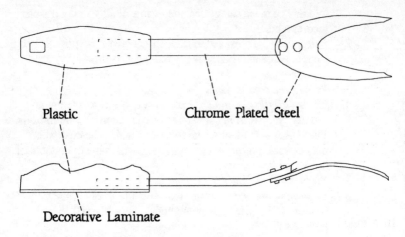

Plastic

Chrome Plated Steel

Decorative Laminate

Figure 3.4 A kitchen fork

encourages bad design, i.e. if the design was correct in the first place, value analysis would have nothing to contribute. This ignores the fact that both designs and technology change, and after a time a design is likely to have become sub-optimal even if it was perfect in the first place. For instance, rear-view mirrors in cars used to be screwed to the roof panel, an expensive process involving several fasteners and the drilling of holes. It was only with the development of reliable adhesives that it became possible to glue mirrors to the windscreen.

The following example illustrates the application of value analysis to the design of an everyday object.

The kitchen fork

The fork is illustrated in Figure 3.4.

The manufacturing process for the kitchen fork is as follows:

	Cost	
	Labour	*Materials*
1. Press fork head	1	12
2. Grind fork head	1.5	

	Cost		
	Labour	*Materials*	
3. Drill rivet holes	2		
4. Bend fork head	1		
5. Cut shaft from extruded steel stock	5	13	
6. Drill rivet holes	2		
7. Bend shaft	1		
8. Rivet shaft to head	2	2	
9. Chrome plate shaft	1	5	
10. Mould handle to shaft	2	12	
11. Fix decorative laminate	1	5	
12. Trim	1		
Total	16	49	65

All costs are in pence.

There are obvious inefficiencies in the riveting of the fork to the shaft, and value analysis would concentrate upon this area, since the rivets obviously do not contribute to the use or esteem values of the product. Alternatives include gluing and welding, both of which would eliminate the need for drilling. It is unlikely that adhesive technology is adequate for this application at present, so it would be rejected after a short investigation. Welding is certainly feasible, but may well cost almost as much as riveting.

An attractive alternative would be to consider a one-piece shaft and head, with a possible change in material to stainless steel. Using a single piece of pressed steel would eliminate operations 3, 5, 6, 7, and 8, while the use of stainless steel would eliminate operation 9.

Further consideration shows that the shaft is at present considerably thicker than the head. To produce the whole fork at this thickness would involve casting, which is much more expensive than pressing (which simply involves stamping the shape out of a sheet of steel), and the points of the fork would have to be profiled. If the whole thing is made to the same thickness as the fork head at present, pressing and bending would be easy, but the overall strength would be reduced, possibly to the point of functional failure. Certainly the fork would look cheaper and lose esteem value.

The apparent simplifications rapidly become less attractive as their implications are further investigated. Even the decorative laminate, which certainly adds nothing to the primary function, makes a major contribution to appearance and therefore esteem value.

Value engineering adopts the same approach as value analysis, but applies it during initial design; it thus leads to designs that are more cost effective initially.

The application of these techniques is not universally welcomed. If well applied, they lead to products that are simpler, cheaper to make, and more reliable. However, they also involve the replacement of many components with few, but more complex, components, and of nuts, screws and similar fastenings with adhesives and one-piece mouldings. The net effect is that when things do go wrong, they are not economically repairable. When a failure does occur, the component responsible is either inaccessible, or is so expensive that it is not worth replacing. Whether the consumer gains overall from the trade-off between lower initial cost and possibly longer life on one hand, and higher repair cost on the other, is questionable. What is certain is that it does encourage the tendency towards discarding rather than repairing.

SUMMARY

Product design is relevant to operations mainly to the extent that it influences ease of manufacture. However, as competitive pressure increases, speed to market with new products has become increasingly important. This has resulted in a much closer relationship developing between design and operations.

The sources of design pressure, market pull, technology push, and process re-equipment have been described. Market pull is certainly the most certain of these influences, but waiting for the market is a reactive strategy, and technology push is more likely to give a major competitive advantage.

Simultaneous engineering, in which the design of the process proceeds in parallel with that of the product, can achieve substantial advantage in terms of time to market, but again, it is not without risk.

Design for manufacture was often neglected, but increasingly with the stress on time to market, and on quality and reliability, as issues of competition, it is achieving greater prominence. Indeed simultaneous engineering almost guarantees that design for manufacture is considered. The most important issues here are process capability and reliability.

Finally the principles of value analysis have been described. This is a valuable approach to both the design of new products and the redesign of existing products. Superficially simple, it seeks to ensure that all aspects of design are considered.

QUESTIONS

Take nothing for granted. In looking at any product, particularly if with a view to its purchase, consider its design. Why is it constructed in that manner?

Why does it have those features? How are they relevant to the use you intend to make of it?

FURTHER READING

A useful overview of product design is found in:
Hollins, G. and Hollins, B. (1991) *Total Design,* Pitman.

4 Service design

PRODUCTS AND SERVICES

As we saw in Chapter 2, services differ from products in a number of ways. The most important difference, from an operations viewpoint, is the simultaneity of production and consumption. The design of a product can occur quite independently of its method of production (though this is not necessarily a good policy to follow); but the design of a service unavoidably incorporates the design of the service-providing operation. The two are inextricably linked. While much of what has been said about product design in Chapter 3 is equally applicable to service design, many other issues also need to be considered.

Most of the issues discussed in Chapter 3 are equally relevant to service design: sources of design pressure are the same, design for operations (rather than manufacture) is perhaps even more important, and even value analysis can be successfully applied to services. Rather than go over these issues again, they will be mentioned briefly in passing and this chapter will then deal with the issues that are particular to services.

EFFICIENCY

The earliest attempts to seriously apply operations management principles to services tended to concentrate on efficiency, and more particularly on utilisation of the service facility.

The problems of operating a service with a high level of utilisation are self-evident. One only has to look at a restaurant in the middle of the afternoon; it will probably be shut, unless it is serving afternoon teas, which are a relatively low-profit offering. High variability, and the impossibility of stocking service, make utilisation a key issue if the organisation is to survive.

Three basic strategies have been developed:

- Remove the customer from the process as far as possible. This allows manufacturing methods to be used for those parts of the process where the customer is not involved.

- Use the customer as labour if the customer's presence is unavoidable.

- Increase the flexibility of staffing so that capacity can match demand.

Front office/back shop

This approach seeks to identify the irreducible minimum involvement of the customer, and assigns these activities to the 'front office'. All other activities are carried out away from the customer in the 'back shop', where conventional manufacturing principles can be applied.

A simple example of this approach can be seen in the contrast between the meat section of a supermarket and a conventional butcher. In the supermarket the customer is presented with a selection of precut preweighed and prepackaged meat prepared out of sight in a meat packing factory by specialist process workers. The customer selects the nearest equivalent to his/her requirement. The service content of the transaction is low but the efficiency is high, since the preparation can be done in advance and the prepared meat stocked. In the butchers, the customer can discuss requirements with the staff, receive advice and have the meat cut to his/her precise requirements. The service content of the transaction is high, and the staff require far more skill both in interpersonal relations and in meat preparation, which is frequently carried out in the presence of the customer. As there is little scope for prepreparation, the whole system is subject to demand variation.

There is no doubt about the efficiencies achieved by the front office/back shop division, but the cost in terms of service content, and in terms of deskilling and reducing the job satisfaction of staff, can be high.

Customer as labour

Self-service is widespread, and few activities seem to be completely immune. Most retail activities involve a degree of self-service, but, until recently, interaction with service personnel was necessary on payment (with the notable exception of vending machines). Now, however, even this last bastion of interpersonal interaction is being eroded by technology. Pumps at filling stations will take credit cards, thus eliminating the need for a cashier. One supermarket chain in the UK is currently experimenting with a system where customers check their own goods through the bar code reader and then pay by charge card. While the facility is being offered only to selected customers, the only security back-up is the threat of random inspection.

In retail banking the concept has been carried to its limit. Automatic teller machines dispense cash, statements and balances, and could also allow bill payments, direct debit authorisations and transfers between accounts. Equally, cash and cheques can be paid in through machines. Some home banking systems allow account holders to carry out any transaction by direct interaction with the bank computer. It is no longer necessary to see or speak to a member of the bank staff.

Since the whole concept of self-service operation is based upon using the customer as labour, the non-capital element of capacity varies automatically in proportion to demand. It is usually combined with a rigid front office/back shop division to maximise the efficiencies.

Self-service has advantages for the customer, in that services are frequently available for longer hours, as in banking, and both waiting times and costs are reduced. The disadvantages arise from the relative absence of help and advice and the much greater demands placed upon the skill and knowledge of the customer. Unskilled or incompetent customers not only damage their own service, but often interfere with that of other customers. The customer who is unsure of the procedures may avoid the facility altogether.

Labour flexibility

Service industries tend to rely heavily on part-time staff. This allows them to vary capacity to meet demand, rather than carry excess capacity during off-peak periods. This imposes substantial management problems. The total labour force may be five or more times the equivalent full-time labour force. Staff loyalty tends to be low and therefore turnover is high (as high as 15 times per year in some parts of the licensed trade). Substantial investment in training is not justified because of the few hours worked and the high turnover. The overall effect of this can be an unskilled and uncommitted labour force, which is hardly likely to encourage customer satisfaction. An alternative approach, which has been used in banks and by the Post Office, is to use the same staff for front office and back shop activities. During peak demand times all customer service points can be manned and back shop activities reduced to a minimum. At other times the majority of staff can be engaged in back shop activities, leaving a minimum on customer service. The success of this approach depends upon the availability of sufficient back shop activities which are not time-sensitive, to allow a proper balance to be achieved. It also depends upon the availability of a suitably skilled labour force, willing to work flexibly.

Demand management

As a last resort, all service activities use demand management as a means of improving the match between demand and capacity. This may be very crude, in the form of simply allowing queues to build up (e.g. most retail outlets), or turning customers away (e.g. restaurants, theatres, etc.) More sophisticated methods include the use of appointment systems and reservations, though these do not guarantee full utilisation, since customers frequently renege. (To overcome this problem, restaurants sometimes require a credit card number with the booking, so that they have some chance of recovering the lost revenue.) Airlines overcome this same problem of 'no shows' by overbooking.

The use of price differentials to encourage demand at off-peak times is widespread, but of limited effectiveness. People travel at peak times because their work demands it, they take holidays during the holiday season, and they eat meals at meal-times. Half-price lunches will tempt few customers at 4.00 in the afternoon.

While all of these approaches have led to substantial efficiencies, it is apparent that they do not necessarily lead to 'good' service. Indeed most of the approaches described can be said to lead to poor service. Self-service is no service at all, and part-time and flexible labour are likely to be less competent and well trained. Queuing and appointments are always worse than immediate service.

Effectiveness

If services are all efficient and cheap, how do service organisations compete? How do they differentiate themselves from the rest of the market? One self-service supermarket is much the same as another, and there is certainly nothing to choose between the ATMs of rival banks.

Service quality has become the watchword of many organisations seeking a way out of this dilemma. Effectiveness is concerned with providing the right service – one which will attract customers, retain customers and differentiate the service-provider from other organisations in the same market. This is generally taken to mean a quality service, so the successful service operation is, almost by definition, now considered to be the provider of a high-quality service.

Service quality is a complex issue which has not yet been effectively defined; however, before we consider it in more detail, it is worth considering further the intrinsic complexity of service.

Figure 4.1 illustrates the elements of a typical service. They are not necessarily all present in all services, and they certainly do not carry equal weight, but most are present most of the time.

Taking them in order:

- *Physical product* represents those goods which change hands during the service transaction. In the retail trade they may be the dominant element of the service – we go to the butcher to buy sausage, not to enjoy his conversation or the decor of the shop,

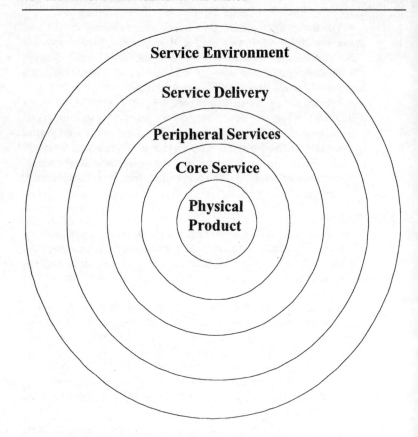

Figure 4.1   Components of a service

but in services such as entertainment, there is little or no physical good to change hands.

- *Core service* represents those elements of the service offering which are essential for its existence, as defined by the service providers. This may be broader than at first sight seems strictly necessary, but it is important that it be clearly defined. A bank offering a current account service might define this as a cheque book and cash card-based service with monthly statements, standing orders, direct debits, offered through a widespread ATM and branch network. Equally, however, it could offer a cash card-based service with monthly statements, free overdraft, interest on credit balances, direct debits, and standing orders, offered through a network of ATMs and 24-hour telephone service. Core service includes the basic mechanisms by which the service is offered.

- *Peripheral services* represent additional elements intended to make the service more attractive, but they are not essential elements of the service itself. For instance, a garden centre may contain a coffee shop. The core service is the provision of garden materials and equipment, not catering facilities, but customers may welcome the opportunity for rest and refreshment. Some credit card companies provide 'free' insurance for purchased goods, and most provide 'free' accident insurance on travel bookings. Some run holiday discount clubs and others run gift schemes. All these extras are peripheral to the core service of providing a payment and budgeting facility.

- *Service delivery* represents the way in which the service is actually provided. It represents the service encounter itself, and the 'script' followed by the customer contact staff. It may be formal and impersonal, or friendly; it may be restrained or obtrusive. One way of distinguishing between this and the core and peripheral services is to think in terms of services – what is offered, and service – the way it is offered. The script for a normal encounter in a self-service restaurant is minimal and may involve little more than the cashier giving the total price. In a waiter service restaurant, opportunities for discussion of the meal alternatives may be provided, but even here there is room for variation – help may be given in a formal and restrained manner, or a friendly and enthusiastic manner. It is in this area that there is the most room for confusion and error. The enthusiastic amateur waiter who might fit perfectly into a lively ethnic restaurant would be very out of place in a formal 'silver service' restaurant.

- *Service environment* represents the physical environment within which the service takes place – its location, size, access, decor, ambience, physical facilities; but it also represents the organisational environment within which the service is offered, recruitment and training policies, staff policies, reward systems, control systems, etc.

For a service to succeed each of these elements must be specified and controlled, and the overall balance must be maintained. This may seem obvious, but it is not easy. The vision of the core service within the firm may be different from that of the market. All too often, the internal environment is not matched to the core service.

The core service of the financial services industry could be defined as offering high-quality investment advice for those seeking to maximise future assets and protect their dependants. This would seem to indicate a need for skilled, knowledgeable, independent advisors, yet the internal service environment is frequently characterised by a reward system based upon commission, which is paid long before the suitability of the advice becomes apparent. This is not to say that financial advisors are driven only by commission, but the reward system is certainly not consistent with the core service requirements. A more consistent service design might have avoided the controversies surrounding the sale of pensions and endowment insurance-based mortgages in the UK in recent times.

A further complication arises from the varying needs and perceptions of different segments of the market. Research into the supermarket trade has found that the elderly do not wish to be rushed, and perceive shopping at least in part as a social opportunity. Most other shoppers see it as a chore to be got over quickly, and certainly do not want to be stuck in a queue while other customers pass the time of day with the checkout operator. The elderly, for this reason, are often more likely to shop early in the week. Again the elderly are far less likely to be concerned about the availability of ATMs in retail banking, and are much more concerned about receiving friendly and respectful treatment in bank branches. A service organisation can seek to please all its customers – there is no reason why a bank should not have both an extensive ATM network and friendly and respectful staff – but recognising the differences and preserving the balance is often difficult.

Perhaps the greatest difficulty arises from market drift. Order-winning criteria, which initially might give competitive advantage, eventually become entry criteria, which are simply essential to attract customers at all. When all garden centres have coffee shops, the coffee shop confers no advantage, but it cannot now be abandoned. More significantly, quality in the core service tends to move from order-winning to entry criteria as it improves, exactly as has happened with products. Again in retail banking, some banks offer financial compensation automatically if they make a mistake, but research has shown that some customers would consider this to be no more than a bribe to accept poor quality, and would expect a bank not to make mistakes at all.

SERVICE QUALITY

Service quality is thus seen as a key issue in achieving competitive advantage in the service sector, and increasingly in the manufacturing sector as buyers increasingly come to expect an overall package from their suppliers.

Defining service quality, however, is not easy. Product quality can be reasonably defined as 'conformance to specification'. There is, in fact, a three-stage process involved, covering three different aspects of quality:

- *Design* The degree to which the product or service meets the needs of the market – fitness for purpose.

- *Conformance* The degree to which the operations system provides products or services which meet specification – conformance to specification.

- *Operational* The degree to which the process produces products or services which meet specification without failure – right first time.

These aspects are frequently not explicitly differentiated in manufacturing, though they are widely recognised. In the service sector this recognition is largely absent, and the result is a considerable amount of confusion.

Again, in the service sector, the customer is the ultimate judge of quality. A dissatisfied customer has had a poor quality service, regardless of whether or not there was a failure in the service-providing system.

A frequent source of complaint about the quality of service in retail banking is problems with direct debits. If a direct debit is wrongly, or unexpectedly, taken from an account, the bank is usually blamed. This is despite the fact that the customer has quite probably signed a direct debit mandate giving the receiving organisation the absolute right to remove money from the account whenever they wish. The bank has no right to intervene.

Banks are not altogether blameless; they do after all promote direct debits, but in this case they unjustly bear the full blame. Protest would, however, do them little good since the first reaction of the customer is to blame the bank.

Most of the work on measuring service quality has been carried out through market research, and a widely accepted definition is:

quality = perception − expectation.

In other words, if the customer experiences a 'better' service than expected, the service is of good quality. This has led to a whole raft of instruments for measuring customer perception, the best known of which is the SERVQUAL instrument developed by Zeithaml, Parasaruman and Berry. This uses two questionnaires, one to measure expectation and another to measure perception. It divides quality into five sections: tangibles, reliability, responsiveness, assurance and empathy, and each of the 22 questions on the questionnaire is associated with one of these sections. Regular use of the instrument is said to allow the gap between perception and expectation to be measured and monitored.

This approach suffers from a number of disadvantages, however:

- The questions are not necessarily universally applicable. Some are irrelevant to some services, while important issues may be missing. Many variations of SERVQUAL have been developed to overcome this, but they do not necessarily then conform to the five aspects, and the generality of the instrument is lost.

- The questions do not necessarily reflect the concerns of customers. A universal problem with the questionnaire is that answers will only be obtained to the questions asked. This, coupled with the fact that the meaning of the question to the respondent might be quite different to that intended by the questionnaire designer suggests that such data must be treated with caution. As an example of the bias introduced by the questions, if supermarket shoppers are asked what is important to them in choosing a supermarket, they are likely to mention price, choice, convenience, value for money. However, if they are given a questionnaire that mentions hygiene or cleanliness, this is likely to be ranked very high, if not first, yet this only really influences buyer behaviour if it is poor.

- The idea that good quality consists in exceeding customer expectations is self-defeating. Given that expectations are, at least in part, determined by previous experience, a good quality service will raise expectations. This of course means that an even better performance will be necessary to register the same perception of quality next time. A continuous spiral of increasing quality is implied.

- Perhaps worst of all, the evidence that good quality, as measured by the perception of customers, actually leads to greater retention and increased market share is not clear. There is some evidence to suggest that the customer's perception of the barriers to change has a bearing on the effect of poor quality. In the UK, bank customers seem to believe that changing banks is difficult, so they complain about poor service but do nothing about it. On the other hand, people change their motor insurance companies at the drop of a discount, regardless of the quality of service offered.

In seeking to design a good quality service, it is necessary to distinguish between the *services* (what is the customer actually buying?), the *service* (the manner in which those core services are provided and the ancillary services used to support them), and the quality of operation of the service-providing system.

If the core and peripheral services are well specified, the market is homogeneous, or at least segmented in a way that is clear and obvious, and the standards of performance can be specified objectively, then there is no real excuse for a service failing. Services do fail, however, for some of the following reasons.

- *Inappropriate core service* The world is littered with good ideas that failed. In many cases this is because only the inventor thought the idea was good. Inappropriate core services do not usually survive long enough to be noticed, but sometimes they are overtaken by events. The mobile shop was an excellent service concept, until it was overtaken by the mobile consumer as car ownership expanded.

- *Inappropriate peripheral services* A pizza chain in the USA invested massively in video and computer games and animatronic displays, with the intention of providing entertainment to diners. The investment was on such a scale that it was unclear whether it was an amusement arcade offering food, or a pizza restaurant offering entertainment. The result was a confused clientele – those who wished to eat were distracted by the games, while those who wished to play did not wish to be surrounded by people eating pizza. The concept failed.

- *Inappropriate service delivery* A motor dealer in the UK carried out market research that showed that while 70 per cent of customers entering the showroom intended to buy a car, only 15 per cent actually did. They concluded that the service delivery, i.e. the car sales staff, was causing customer loss, and retrained staff to stop selling. Staff instead became advisers, helping customers to articulate their needs and evaluate the alternatives on offer. The result was an increase in the conversion rate from 15 per cent to 35 per cent.

- *Inappropriate service environment* As any marketer will tell you, location is one of the most important decisions for a service outlet. A high-class grocer in the middle of a deprived housing estate will not succeed. Small businesses frequently get their location wrong, usually due to the triumph of optimism over common sense. While a feature may occasionally be made of an inappropriate environment – one public house in London used to claim not to have cleaned or decorated the premises for over 100 years – the standard of decor, space, furnishings, etc. is again usually obvious, if not always affordable. It is the internal environment that is more usually inappropriate. Where customer needs are objective and predictable, customer service staff will not be expected to exercise discretion; training, control and support systems can be mechanistic and management structures rigidly hierarchical. A supermarket checkout operator needs manual dexterity and an ability to handle money; if there is a problem they summon a supervisor. Where customer needs are more complex and where the judgement about the quality of the outcome is more subjective, customer service staff need interpersonal skills and discretion. Such people need careful selection and training, but they also need support and control systems which value their contribution and treat them as responsible members of the team. Taking the example of the car retailers mentioned above, if the company had maintained a control system based upon individual commission and sales targets, then the change from sales to advice would have failed, because the signals from the system would still have shown selling as the main objective. Instead, the control systems were changed to operate on a group bonus system over a longer time horizon.

How can we ensure that our service is good? There is, as yet, no established approach. Value analysis can certainly be applied. Each element of the service and each step in the service process is identified and analysed, and alternatives considered in the same way as for product design. The most important element in the process, however, is to maintain a customer viewpoint.

SUMMARY

While product and service design share much common ground, there are important differences assopciated with the service characteristics identified in Chapter 2.

Early attempts at applying operations design principles to services – the industrialisation of services – led to a stress on efficiency that was intended to counteract the variability of demand and the volatility of services. It was subsequently found that almost all attempts to improve service efficiency led to a deterioration in the service. While this is of little importance when services are competing on cost, the increasing competition in the market place has led to a quest for other competitive competencies.

Quality has been identified as a key competitive differentiator in many services; however, quality is ill-defined in products, and even more vague in services. Several models of service quality exist and two have been described, together with the many ways in which service quality can fail.

In summary, although service quality is seen as the most important competitive issue by many service-providers, it is poorly defined and its influence on customer retention unproven.

QUESTIONS

As with products, consider the design of any service you experience. Is it obvious what your role is? Are the facilities and staff consistent with the service expected? Are there features of the service that are inappropriate?

Again using your example organisation, what service does it provide to its customers? How customer-centred is it? How much does it take for granted?

FURTHER READING

In addition to Normann (see Chapter 2), the following give a useful, if academic insight into service quality:

Rust, R. T. and Oliver, R. L. (eds) (1994) *Service quality: New Directions in Theory and Practice,* Sage.

Zeithaml, V. A., Parasuraman, A. and Berry, L. L. (1990) *Delivering Quality Service. Balancing Customer Perceptions and Expectations*, The Free Press.

The following are of more general interest:

Collier, D. A. (1994) *The Service/Quality Solution,* Irwin.

Schmenner, R. W. (1995) *Service Operations Management,* Prentice Hall.

5 Processes 1: The quest for efficiency

> Musrum frequently complained that he never had enough time, and what little he had was of the very poorest quality.
>
> *Earnshaw and Thacker (1968)*

INTRODUCTION

Operations as a discipline has its roots in the scientific management school. While many of these concepts are very old (see Appendix 1), most developed during the latter part of the nineteenth century, and continue to be refined and elaborated.

The driving force throughout has been a mix of profit and market share, so the pressure on operations has been minimisation of cost, maximisation of efficiency and utilisation. The most important contribution has perhaps been the hierarchic organisational structures that have built up as a result of the principle of the division of labour, and this will be considered first. Following that, a number of the more significant issues concerned with the efficient management of operations will be considered.

What follows is primarily concerned with manufacturing operations, but parallels will be seen with the early development of service operations and the quest for utilisation, described in the previous chapter.

55

DIVISION OF LABOUR

An important element in the early development of scientific management was the idea of the division of labour. While a craftsman can produce a product of high quality without supervision or 'management', this process is inefficient. Many of the tasks carried out are trivial, and could be carried out by lower-grade (and lower-cost) labour, and a great deal of time is spent starting up and stopping activities. For instance, consider the manufacture of a three-legged stool in timber. The processes are:

- Cut legs to length.
- Turn legs to shape.
- Sand legs to an acceptable smoothness.
- Cut seat.
- Shape seat.
- Drill holes for locating legs.
- Sand.
- Glue legs to seat.
- Varnish.

A craftsman may well make a single stool from start to finish, involving frequent changes of position, moving from one machine or work area to another, getting out and putting away tools and materials, setting up and stripping down machines. The proportion of effort spend on peripheral activities rather than direct productive work could be as high as 75 per cent.

A scientific appraisal and analysis of the process identifies essential and peripheral tasks. It becomes quite obvious that the way to reduce the peripheral tasks is to concentrate the essential tasks in some way to avoid the need for frequent changes. Thus many legs are cut to length, and only when they are all cut does the operator move on to turning the legs. Instead of a change of activity with each stool, there is a change with each batch of 100, or whatever number is deemed appropriate. Division of labour takes this approach even further. There is no need for the operator to change to the next stage for every batch, if a separate operator is used for each stage. This almost completely eliminates changeover time. It also leads to more skilled operators, since they gain far more practice, but since the operator is now carrying out only one, predefined, task, s/he can no longer claim to be a craftsman, so the rate of pay is lower. The proportion of effort spent on peripheral activities may be reduced to 25 per cent or less.

Division of labour thus divides tasks into many relatively small, specialised units. It imposes a requirement for standardisation, since the worker does not follow the work through the process. It also demands planning and co-ordination, so it involves a division between labour and management, and between line management, who are responsible for ensuring that labour carry out the requisite activities, and staff who are responsible for the design and planning of those activities. The end product is the fully developed functionally divided hierarchical organisation. The ultimate application of this approach is sometimes referred to as **Taylorism**, after Frederick Taylor, or as **Fordism**, after Henry Ford and the development of the flow line (see Appendix).

The structure of the modern manufacturing organisation can be traced directly to this simple concept. The subdivision of the

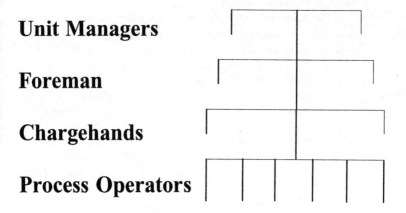

Figure 5.1 Manufacturing line management structure

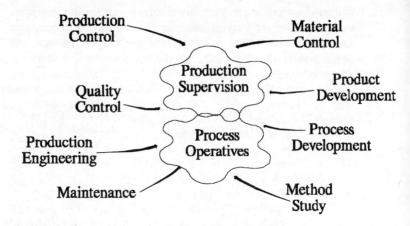

Figure 5.2 Manufacturing support services

workforce into discrete sections carrying out limited tasks creates the
need for co-ordination and management. As scale and variety
increase, so the support and management functions become divided
into more and more specialisms. In manufacturing, as well as the line
management hierarchy shown in Figure 5.1, we have the support
services shown in Figure 5.2.

This fragmentation of the management role introduces a further
need for co-ordination, and so we see the **organisation and methods**
and the **information systems** specialists as well as financial control,
manpower planning and strategic planning functions.

In general, it can be argued that this functional specialisation
allows large, complex, multi-activity organisations to exist. No one
person can possibly perform all the activities that are necessary for
a modern manufacturing organisation to function. In theory, the use
of specialists, whether in operating a machine, or in financial
planning, greatly enhances both the effectiveness and efficiency of
the organisation. People can get on with their tasks with less
interruption and fewer changeovers, and, since they are expert, they
will perform the task accurately and efficiently. The effects of this
structure, however, are not all positive. Each new functional division
carries with it an overhead in terms of demands upon the systems of

the organisation, and in pure labour terms – a department needs a department head to manage it. It is much more difficult to maintain an overall vision of the purpose of the organisation; departments begin to behave as if they are ends in themselves, rather than means to achieve organisational goals. The following vignette illustrates this type of problem.

David Allen, production manager of Electronic Components' heavy duty factory, was worried. Demand had been well down on budget for the winter quarter but he had been able to avoid short-time working by bringing forward orders for delivery in the spring quarter. Without a miracle, he would probably have to lay people off in the spring, but a more pressing concern was the end of quarter stock report. As a result of making early he was going to be at least 70 per cent above budget on finished goods stock.

One order in particular, for Power Distribution PLC, a major customer, accounted for most of the excess stock, but the order specified clearly that it must not be delivered before the middle of the spring quarter. Despite this he decided to approach Jonathan Livingstone, his sales manager, with the proposal that it be shipped early.

Jonathan was surprisingly enthusiastic. Because of the recession, he was well below target on orders shipped, and delivering this order early would greatly improve the figures. He called in Annette McDonald, who was responsible for the Power Distribution contracts and asked her opinion.

Annette: 'They made it very clear that they did not want anything shipped early. They do not have the warehouse space and they are certainly not going to pay for early delivery.'

Jonathan: 'Yes but what would they actually do if we shipped early? Would they cancel the order or what?'

Annette: 'They would complain vigorously, they wouldn't pay until 90 days after the date they wanted delivery, they might even send it back, but I don't think they would cancel.'

Jonathan: 'We'll risk it then. David, you ship on the last day of the quarter and if they complain we will blame it on clerical error.'

The order was duly shipped and both sales and production were near budget for the quarter. A week later the order was returned by Power Distribution. It was then shipped out on the required delivery date and so figured in the spring quarter sales budget as well.

The behaviour of the protagonists is quite sensible in terms of their need to meet functional objectives, but is damaging to the organisation as a whole.

Functionally divided organisations suffer from slow communication, information frequently has to ascend through one branch of the hierarchy before descending through another – a salesman does not talk to a production foreman directly. Lack of visibility of the whole can lead to lack of loyalty to the organisation, and low motivation.

THE ROLE OF INVENTORY

In manufacturing, inventory allows the production operation to be isolated from the vagaries both of the market and of suppliers. Production can be carried out with the maximum efficiency, if it does not have to respond to changes in demand, or problems of supply.

In the service sector, the greater the degree of industrialisation, through maximising the back shop operation, the more stock can be used as a buffer against the much greater variation in demand.

Stock is not without its problems, most of which can be expressed as a cost – the cost of holding stock can be as great as 30 per cent of its value per year. The cost of running out of stock can vary from the fairly trivial (buying stationary retail, because of a stockout) to the catastrophic (closing the factory due to a shortage of raw material, or running out of blood in the middle of a surgical operation). Another cost associated with stock is the fixed cost of setting up to manufacture the item.

A company manufactures cardboard cartons. The first stage in the process is cutting the card to shape. This is followed by printing, then folding and gluing. Each time a different product is to be manufactured, it takes about an hour to set up the cutting machine for that product at a cost of about £120 in materials, labour and overheads.

While set-up cost is obvious in manufacturing, it also applies when buying in materials – the administrative cost of sending an order to a supplier can be about £30. In many service activities such costs are largely independent of the number of customers. For example, an evening class in holiday Spanish costs the same to run for 30 people as for one, and a 300-seat airliner costs much the same to operate whether empty or full. These situations are analogous with the factory set up.

Economic batch quantity

The main approach of the scientific management school is the conduct of experiments to determine the 'best' way to do something. In many cases these experiments can be set up through the use of mathematical models, rather than the much more difficult and expensive approach of manipulating the real world. The **economic batch quantity** is one of the most widely used models. For a given level of output in a time period (say a year), there is a wide choice of possible batch sizes, ranging from a hand-to-mouth operation, only making what is immediately required, through to making a whole year's requirement (or more) at once. Obviously the larger the individual batch size, the fewer set-ups per year, and the lower the total set-up cost; however, the result of large batch sizes is large stockholding and a higher stockholding cost. The economic batch quantity is the batch size that exactly matches the total cost of set-up with the total cost of stockholding for a particular product or service. It is illustrated graphically in Figure 5.3.

This example illustrates a general procedure whereby the various sources of cost (and revenue, if relevant) are established, and mathematical formulae are set up to model them. These formulae are then manipulated to give an optimal (best) answer.

In the real world, of course, the EBQ is only the starting point, and restrictions of cost, availability of space, shelf-life of the product, and even fashion might suggest that smaller quantities than optimal should be bought/made. It is, however, a very good starting point.

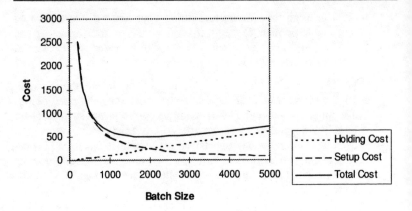

Figure 5.3 Economic batch quantity

Safety stocks

The EBQ balances the costs of stockholding and procurement, but does not address the cost of stockout. In an ideal world, a new batch would be ordered/manufactured so that it would become available just as the last batch was used up. In practice, both supply and demand are too unpredictable for this to be possible, so the new consignment is programmed to arrive while there is, normally, still some stock remaining. This stock is the **safety stock** and is intended to allow for higher than average demand and longer than average delivery times. The chance, and therefore the long-term cost, of stockout can be reduced by holding more safety stock, but this puts up the cost of stockholding. The position is exactly equivalent to the EBQ, in that one cost rises as another falls, and there will therefore be an optimal safety stockholding for any given situation. This argument applies even in the case of safety-critical situations – for example, stocks of blood – since one can never be certain that the maximum possible demand has been allowed for.

Unfortunately it is rarely possible to establish with any confidence the real cost of stockout, since it could include loss of future business if a customer becomes very disenchanted. Precise mathematical modelling is replaced by subjective judgement, and the safety stock is set at a level that will guarantee a specified level of service. A 95 per cent service level system is one that will meet all demand 95 per cent of the time.

THE PROBLEM OF SCHEDULING

In total, scheduling involves two stages:

1. converting actual, or forecast, demand for products or services into demand for labour and plant resources;
2. specifying precisely when particular products or services will be processed with precisely which resources.

This is best illustrated with a simple example.

> Premium Printers supply printed circuit boards to specialist manufacturers of electronic equipment. Most orders are for only a few tens or hundreds of boards, and orders are rarely repeated. Manufacture is a simple five-stage process, starting with bought-in copper laminated board:
>
> 1. The circuit pattern is printed onto the copper surface in acid resistant wax.
> 2. The remaining copper is dissolved in an acid bath, followed immediately by a wash to remove acid.
> 3. The wax is removed in a solvent bath.
> 4. The required component contact holes are drilled.
> 5. The board is inspected and packed for shipment.
>
> Orders are usually processed as discrete batches. Only printing and drilling involve significant set-up.

In order to match capacity, the input of resources, to output, it is necessary to have a common unit of measurement. With single-product manufacture this can be almost anything – for example, a sugar mill can define its capacity in terms of tonnes of sugar year, tonnes of beet processed per year, or even £000 revenue per year, if the price is stable. Where different products are produced, possibly using some common and some different facilities, the only useful measure of capacity is available time. One operator running one machine has a capacity of 37 hours in a standard week, which may be enough to process 100 of one product or 1,000 of another. Time available is the common denominator.

For Premium Printers to plan output, a database containing the time required for each stage of each product is required. This would be developed from some form of work measurement. Large organisations would use trained work measurement engineers to set up and continuously maintain this database, but a small firm like Premium Printers would normally rely on experience and the occasional check.

New orders, or updated forecasts, are converted into demand for time at the process stages involved. They can then be scheduled, that is matched to the available time, and a completion date established. This can be given to the customer as a delivery promise, or if earlier delivery is required, additional capacity might be obtained by working overtime, delaying less urgent work or subcontracting.

The database containing the necessary information is often referred to as the **bill of materials**; in addition to the process stages and times for each process it would also include material and component requirements.

Provided the bill of materials is accurate, there should be no great difficulty in converting demand for products into demand for capacity; the problem arises when converting demand for capacity into an efficient and workable schedule. If Premium Printers has a forward order book of 20 batches, the only variable available in producing the schedule is the sequence in which the batches are processed. The times required at different stages will vary from batch to batch, but not in a consistent manner. For example one type of board (A) may require seven hours at printing and five at drilling, while another (B) may require four at printing and six at drilling. If board A were processed first, then board B would be ready for drilling by the time board A was finished. If board B were processed first, however, drilling would be idle for at least one hour after completing board B. Depending upon the sequence in which batches are processed, machines may be idle waiting for work for a greater or lesser time. The best schedule is the one which minimises this idle time. Unfortunately, the only way to find the best schedule is by trial and error, and with 20 batches there are 1.8×10^{18} possible schedules. This problem is too large even for modern computers, so a simplifying assumption is frequently used. It is assumed that all batches take a fixed time (one day, or one week) at each process stage.

Now all that is necessary is to specify which orders will go through printing on, say, Monday. These orders can then go through drilling on Tuesday, or later, and so on. The sequence of processing Monday's batches no longer matters, since none are required to be finished before Tuesday.

Independent demand

The fixed period scheduling rule described above effectively uses stock to buffer each process stage from the adjacent stages. When stock is also used to buffer manufacture from supply, through raw material and component stocks, and from demand through finished goods stocks, production as a whole is independent of outside influences. In addition, each process stage is, to a degree, independent of other process stages. It is now possible to optimise the production process so that it runs at maximum efficiency. The procedures involved are relatively simple, and great accuracy of control and recording is unnecessary since the stock buffers are fairly tolerant of error. Not only is labour now divided, but so is detailed planning and control.

The disadvantages of this approach to manufacturing management only became apparent with the changing economic environment of the 1950s. Globalisation and over-capacity in manufacturing led to increasing competition in price, quality and variety. Technological development and greater wealth led to more rapid changes in the market. Higher labour, premises and interest charges led to a rapid escalation in the cost of stock. Independent demand scheduling, with its high stockholding, became much more expensive.

Independent demand scheduling is an intrinsically slow system with a very high inertia. A production process with 20 process stages may have a 20-week throughput time. This, when coupled with six weeks' raw material stock and six weeks' finished goods stock, means that it takes at least 32 weeks to respond to a change in demand. Such inertia is a serious threat to survival.

THE TECHNOLOGICAL FIX

The development of computer technology coincided with the

realisation that independent demand scheduling was no longer adequate. The computer would enable the intrinsic complexity of the scheduling problem to be managed in a way that would reduce stock and throughput time. The solution was eventually to be realised in the guise of **manufacturing resources planning** (usually called MRP II, the II distinguishing it from its predecessor, material requirements planning).

The American Production and Inventory Control Society defines MRP II as:

> A method for the effective planning of all resources of a manufacturing company. Ideally, it addresses operational planning in units, financial planning in dollars, and has simulation capability to answer 'what if' questions. It is made up of a variety of functions, each linked together: business planning, capacity requirements planning, master production scheduling, material requirements planning, and the execution of support systems for capacity and material. Output from these systems would be integrated with financial reports such as the business plan, purchase commitment report, shipping budget, inventory projections, etc.

Few, if any, organisations have implemented a complete and comprehensive MRP II system, but aspects of it are widely used. The basic principle behind this approach is to treat demand at all stages of the process as dependent upon demand at succeeding stages, as it actually is. The simplifying assumption of independence has proved too expensive, so it must be abandoned.

In an ideal world this is not particularly difficult. Lead times are added to the bill of materials database – not only for purchased materials and components, but also for each process stage. The process stage lead times can be left at one week, but greater efficiency is achieved if they are shortened. The schedule is now built up by working backwards from required delivery dates, so that the latest time for each process to start is specified, as well as the time when the necessary materials should be ordered.

For example, an order for 100 circuit boards for delivery in week 20 would lead to a schedule as follows:

Week	Action
20	Deliver
19	Inspect and pack
18	Drill
17	Etch and clean
16	Print
12	Order board

This schedule is based upon a four-week lead time for the board and a one-week process lead time. (If a one-day process lead time were used, then the total lead time would be reduced from eight weeks to five weeks.) This is fine as long as it is not yet week 12, and as long as the capacity is actually available to carry out the work when specified. In this case stock is no longer required and responsiveness is greatly improved.

The reality is usually sadly different. Customer requirements may demand a more rapid response than the total lead time, so the manufacturing plan must be based upon forecast, not actual, demand. This means stock accumulates when forecasts are not met, and safety stocks must be kept to allow for demand in excess of forecast. Firm orders may be changed, leading to part-finished stock, and suppliers may not be reliable enough, so raw material stocks must still be kept. MRP does not, in fact eliminate stock. It actually makes its control much more complex, and, because it is driven by actual orders for products, it demands much more accurate recording of stock at all stages of the process. Effective MRP II really requires factory floor on-line data collection and a highly disciplined work force.

The problem of matching the schedule to available capacity is managed by carrying out a rough capacity-matching stage before the detailed schedule is produced. However, even with this, it is sometimes necessary to go back to the beginning and alter the delivery schedule when the final detailed schedule is found to exceed available capacity.

MRP II *can* work. It leads to faster throughput, lower stock and greater responsiveness. It is, however, expensive. It requires considerable investment in computer hardware and software. More importantly, it requires a complete change in attitude for both management and factory floor. Accurate recording, and precise following of the published schedule, are essential. Educating those used to the tolerant atmosphere of an independent demand system is probably even more difficult and expensive than implementing the computer system.

THE ISRAELI ALTERNATIVE

An alternative approach, developed by Goldratt, overturns one of the basic assumptions of the classical scientific management approach to operations.

The fundamental assumption of the foregoing methods is that:

$$profit = revenue - cost$$

and

$$cost\ per\ unit = cost\ per\ hour/output\ per\ hour$$

This is no doubt true for the production unit as a whole. The insight that led to the development of the approach, which is variously known as optimised production technology (OPT), theory of constraints and synchronous manufacture, was that only goods shipped actually generate revenue. Output at individual process stages only affects profit if it affects output from the whole system.

Most production processes have bottlenecks, or constraints – production stages where the capacity may be less than the overall demand. Other production stages have excess capacity. OPT recognises that utilisation is only critical at bottlenecks, since excess output at non-constrained stages merely generates stock, not revenue.

This gives rise to a number of significant consequences.

- Batch sizes at bottlenecks are based upon a set-up cost that includes the value of lost output during the set-up (if output is genuinely constrained at this stage, then revenue could be being generated during the set-up time), but batch sizes at non-constrained stages may be much smaller. Batch identity is not preserved through the process.

- Scheduling is only really a problem at bottlenecks. All other process stages have spare capacity. The production of 'good' if not optimal schedules is much easier if there are only a few process stages to consider – at the limit, a procedure called Johnson's Algorithm can be used to produce an optimal schedule if only two process stages are involved – so OPT leads to more optimal schedules since only the, hopefully few, bottlenecks need to be considered in detail.

- Performance monitoring and budget systems based upon utilisation of individual process stages are no longer relevant. The control and reward systems, and management attitudes, of an organisation implementing OPT need to change.

Like MRP, the OPT scheduling process takes projected delivery dates and schedules completions back from this, but only bottlenecks are scheduled on the first pass. This schedule is then adjusted to match capacity if necessary, and then non-constrained processes are scheduled forward.

Again like MRP, the implementation of OPT depends upon purchasing the necessary computer hardware and software, then embarking upon an extensive implementation and training process. It is not a cheap solution to the problem of scheduling.

QUALITY

The scientific method paradigm sees quality as a problem to be solved, and applies the concept of optimality to it. The process should be designed and operated to conform with the design quality specification, but there will be a cost associated with achieving high quality, just as there is a cost associated with failure. The situation is analogous to that of the economic batch quantity. Somewhere there as an optimal trade-off between the design of the process to achieve conformance, the use of inspection to reduce non-conformance, and the shipping of defective products to the customer.

The classical approach to the problem is embodied in **statistical quality control**. This is based upon the use of rigidly designed sampling schemes to test output for conformance. It accepts that non-conformance is inevitable, and balances the cost of non-conformance against the cost of inspection. Inspection is usually carried out by a separate team of inspectors who report to a chief inspector quite independently of operations. This ensures impartiality, but often leads to a situation where inspection is seen as the opposition, and the cause of quality problems.

Statistical process control uses similar principles of sampling, but is applied early in the process to ensure that the process is operating correctly.

SUMMARY

The scientific management paradigm has a long and successful history. It has been the mainstay of the industrial revolution, and the subsequent global industrialisation; however it worked best when demand exceeded capacity, when everything that was made could be sold. As globalisation of markets has increased, and global manufacturing capacity has exceeded demand, the scientific management paradigm has struggled to maintain its position and has led to increasingly complex and expensive solutions. These solutions are not untenable, but their complexity renders them fragile, and their high cost reduces their value as means of containing overall manufacturing costs. As we will see in Chapter 6, they are not the only approach.

QUESTIONS

Considering your example organisation or department, how is capacity managed? Is any attempt made to predict work loads and arrange resources to meet planned outputs? Does capacity planning work?

REFERENCE

Earnshaw and Thacker (1968) *Musrum*, Jonathan Cape.

FURTHER READING

For an interesting, quasi-fictional, view of manufacturing operations:
Goldratt, E. M. and Cox, J. (1986) *The Goal*, North River Press.

For an introduction to statistical quality control:

Montgomery, D.C. (1991) *Introduction to Statistical Quality Control*, John Wiley.

The following book gives a very good overview of the contrasts between the scientific management paradigm and the 'Japanese Way' (see Chapter 6):

Cole, W.E. and Mogab, J.W. (1994) *The Economics of Total Quality Management*, Blackwell.

6 Processes 2: The Japanese way

INTRODUCTION

An apparently complex and endless set of approaches and techniques seem to have emerged from Japan since the early 1950s. They share a common basis which is essentially simple pragmatism. It is said that Toyota, in seeking to rebuild its car production facility after the Second World War, modelled its development upon the American example of Detroit. This was a typically stock-heavy, utilisation-driven system, but was, at the time, seen as the way to build cars. Unfortunately Toyota could not afford the stock, so ways had to be found of operating without stock; and so **just in time** (JIT) was born.

The **total quality** approach arose from a similar attack of pragmatism. Early post-reconstruction manufacture in Japan was of poor quality. In America and Europe, following the development of statistical quality control, quality management had become a technical specialism. The Japanese had neither the specialists nor the time for training. Acting under the influence of, among others, Deming – whose ideas were not particularly welcome in his home country, the USA – the idea that quality was everyone's business developed. Again this was a pragmatic response to an immediate need.

JUST IN TIME

The term 'just in time' is widely misused, but it is the term that best encapsulates the outcome of Japanese pragmatism. Far too many organisations still see it as primarily a stock reduction technique, and simply insist upon suppliers delivering materials and components 'just in time' – often several times per shift – to the point of use in the production process. In order to achieve this, the suppliers need to hold even greater stocks of finished goods, and the effect is simply to push stockholding back onto the supplier. The costs of stockholding are still incurred and, overall, there is no improvement in efficiency or effectiveness.

JIT works only if applied to the whole supply chain, and it is obviously easier for an organisation to apply it to its internal operations, rather than trying to impose it upon its suppliers.

A good working definition of the whole JIT philosophy is:

Instant supply of perfect quality, in whatever quantity is required, with zero waste.

This is of course impossible, but the underlying philosophy is one of continuous development and improvement, which does not recognise an end point short of perfection. Unlike the scientific method paradigm, which identifies problems to be solved, JIT identifies situations to be improved, and further improvement is always possible. As a result it requires continuous attention at all levels in the organisation.

The key to JIT is the definition of waste:

Waste is any asset or activity that is not directly contributing to meeting customer needs.

Waste thus includes:

- all stock not being actively worked upon, since it is tying up capital and space nonproductively;
- machine and operator idle time;
- set-up time, since the process is not actually producing during set-up;
- scrap and rework, which are waste by any definition;

- any activities that do not directly contribute to satisfying
customer needs.

Pull scheduling

In manufacturing, the heart of a successful JIT programme is pull
scheduling. Conventional scheduling pushes material through from
the first stage, loading batches onto this and expecting them to
continue through the process. In pull scheduling, however, the final
stage process is only activated in response to a demand for finished
product. The use of material by the final stage then generates demand
for material from the penultimate stage, and so on back to the
suppliers. The control mechanism for this is the *kanban* (Japanese
for card). The kanban may be a card which is used to authorise
production. When it is received by the final stage, that stage
assembles the product from the components it already has. Having
used those components it passes a kanban on to the preceding stage
as a request for more components. Alternatively the kanban may be
a physical container for the components, or a space between stages.
An empty container or space provides the necessary authority for
work to be carried out. A stock-based kanban system is illustrated in
Figure 6.1.

The main effect of this approach is that problems are
immediately apparent. If any process stage encounters problems,
from whatever cause, the whole line stops because subsequent stages
will rapidly run out of material, and preceding stages will run out of
kanbans. Unlike a push scheduling system, earlier stages cannot
continue to build up material for stock. Problems are thus

Four Item Kanban

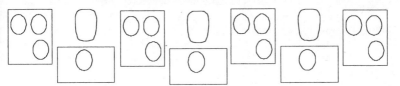

Workstation

Figure 6.1 A three-stage process with a four-item kanban

immediately apparent, and must be solved rather than bypassed. Such a system is very vulnerable: without stock, any delay at any stage will stop production completely. In order to survive at all, a number of prerequisites are required, designed to reduce the risk of failure and the exposure should failure occur.

Total quality

Quality failure is not only anathema because it is waste, it is also to be avoided because it would stop the process. The philosophy that non-productive effort is waste does, of course, identify inspection as an unnecessary activity, and is therefore committed to the concept of 'right first time'. Total quality rejects absolutely the idea that there is an optimum level of failure.

One effect of this is to avoid the dichotomy that is frequently seen in conventional manufacturing plants, where quality is always seen as a problem belonging to somebody else. In a total quality environment, quality is everyone's concern. Workplace based **quality circles** meet regularly to identify quality problems and seek their resolution. All members of staff are encouraged to identify ways of improving quality, whether within their own area of competence or not. Technical support treats all ideas seriously and provides assistance and training to quality circles. All members of staff are seen as inspectors, and are entitled to identify and publicise quality failures.

Total quality depends heavily upon statistical process control, but sampling and measurement are not carried out by experts, but by the direct labour force itself. Everyone is trained in the technique.

Total quality has been widely adopted in the service sector, partly as a way of bypassing the problems of quality definition, and partly because orthodox inspection procedures cannot easily be applied to services.

Preventative maintenance

Plant failure is as damaging as material failure, and well designed and controlled preventative maintenance programmes are essential for successful pull scheduling. The objective is to avoid failure during use by ensuring plant is always in excellent condition.

Process redesign

Small production units are essential in JIT for several reasons:

- *Motivation* The team approach implicit in quality circles and in *kaizen* (see below) requires a sense of identity among staff which is more likely to develop if all stages are visible to each other. Small U-shaped units are usually best for this.

- *Vulnerability* Since any failure will stop the whole unit, small units reduce the exposure of the organisation as a whole.

- *Transport* Transport of goods is wasteful of space and time; small units reduce transport requirements.

Balanced flow is equally necessary since bottlenecks imply wasted capacity at other stages. It is generally easier to balance a small unit with relatively few process stages.

Set-up time is to be reduced and if possible eliminated. The constraints of the economic batch quantity still apply in JIT plants, so a great deal of design and engineering effort is devoted to reducing set-up times. This frequently means extensive in-house redesign of manufacturing plant.

The system must be robust. It must not be prone to failure. This means that JIT units do not usually use very advanced technology, and are likely to be a few years behind the technological leaders in the field.

Flexible labour

In order to cope with variations in output, and with the inevitable failures that will occur, labour within a JIT unit is often expected to be able to operate any of the processes. Equally they are responsible for cleaning, routine maintenance, etc. In the event of a problem causing the unit to stop, everyone would be expected to assist in its solution. Those not actively engaged in problem-solving would carry out such housekeeping tasks as were necessary.

Product design

To achieve the full effect of small balanced production units, some product redesign is frequently required. This is frequently in line with the waste-reduction philosophy, in that unnecessary variety and complexity are eliminated; however, there is a risk of conflict between the goal of eliminating variety to simplify production, and meeting customer requirements.

JIT purchasing

Having components of perfect quality delivered by the supplier, two or three times a shift, to the point of use obviously saves space and other stockholding costs. Provided the supplier is also operating JIT, it does not merely push the costs further back in the supply chain. To be effective, the system requires a high degree of trust and substantial sharing of information. Suppliers must also be operating total quality, and they must have direct access to changes in the master production schedule.

JIT also requires fairly close proximity of supplier and customer, and reliable transport. Some Japanese manufacturers are now moving away from this concept because of the very high costs of transport in the more congested parts of Japan. Transport costs, if significant, must be included in the economic batch quantity calculation.

THE BENEFITS OF JIT

The main benefits of JIT arise from reduced costs, increased responsiveness and greater quality.

Cost reduction arises from the reduction in resources required for manufacture, and the reduction in scrap and rework. This will vary with the starting point, but the aim should be to eliminate all costs due to scrap and rework, as well as the cost of operating an inspection function. Some of this saving may be ploughed back into maintaining the total quality process. The following case illustrates the potential for other savings.

> Premium Products produce a range of electrical components used in the manufacture of domestic appliances. Until last year they used a conventional batch manufacturing process. Despite implementing MRP three years ago, they found that they still had an average of four weeks' material and component stock. In addition, because they were using a one-week time bucket, the average process lead time was nine

weeks. While much production was to order, finished goods stocks still averaged six weeks' sales.

In total, stockholding was valued at £16m. on a turnover of £80m. (direct cost of £50m.), made up as follows:

Finished goods	50 x 6/52	= 6
Raw material	50 x 4 x 0.7/52	= 3 (raw material represented about 70% of total cost)
Work in progress	50 x 9 x 0.85/52	= 7

This stockholding was costing the company £2.8m. per year in finance charges alone.

JIT was progressively implemented by reducing batch sizes and reducing the MRP time bucket at the same time. It was found that some products could be grouped together and removed from the MRP system altogether, since they formed a balanced output at normal usage rates. The cost of new and redesigned plant and revised layouts in the first year amounted to £0.8m., while increased wages, a necessary step to obtain staff commitment, cost a further £0.7m.

Since the average work content of the product range was 64 hours, the potential reduction in work in progress stock, on the typical 50-hour week, is 86 per cent, or £6m. The reduction after one year was £3.8m., with a further reduction in finished goods stock of £1.9m. The saving in finance charges thus amounts to £1m. per year, which, given the increased labour cost, is a net saving of £0.3m. This, however, is early days, and the stock reduction is expected to at least double within the next twelve months. The company is still trying to find a use for the floor space now unused, amounting to 19 per cent of total production floor area.

THE DISADVANTAGES OF JIT

JIT, as a philosophy, has no obvious disadvantages. It can be applied to any situation, the objective being to identify and eliminate all sources of delay and waste. As exemplified by pull scheduling, however, there are obvious limitations. Pull scheduling only works if the supply chain has been primed with the necessary components to meet the final demand. If the final stage is asked to produce a blue widget, but the previous kanban contains the components for a green widget, the system collapses. In other words, a constant planned pattern of demand is necessary. It is certainly possible to work a schedule that is no longer appropriate through the system much more quickly than in a conventional batch environment, but it must still be done. Perfect JIT requires perfect demand forecasts.

DEVELOPMENTS FROM JIT

A number of developments in the organisation of operations can be traced back to the effect that JIT has had on conventional management thinking. Some of these are outlined below.

Kaizen

Total quality, though initially developed to compensate for a lack of quality experts, and then used to ensure the necessary zero defects for a pull scheduling system, goes well beyond the idea of component and product meeting specification. The kaizen approach makes small teams responsible, not only for the management and allocation of their work, but also for the quality of that work and for the quality of the process. It has a strong emphasis on continuous improvement.

The use of small teams, with nominated team leaders to manage and operate particular production units, is a characteristic of lean manufacture, and the key to de-layering. The lean organisation delegates decision-making to the lowest level, and eliminates the intermediate management layers. It can be seen as an extension of the general philosophy of waste reduction to the hierarchy of the organisation, but it really stems from the empowered team nature of quality circles.

Kaizen is not without its problems. It has been suggested that some organisations have de-layered to the extent that they are not so much lean as emaciated, and the problems of executive stress are increasingly being found on the shop floor.

Partnership

JIT supply forces the partnership concept onto the upstream side of the supply chain. The need to establish co-operation and trust with suppliers forces a reduction in the number of suppliers that a company can afford to deal with. A natural consequence of partnership in current activities is shared technology and management methods. If the customer can help the supplier become more efficient, everyone benefits.

Further development of the relationship leads to **simultaneous engineering**, or black box design. With this approach, in new product development, the supplier is asked to design components to meet particular functions, rather than being asked to manufacture to a defined specification. This improves design quality by harnessing suppliers' design expertise, and speeds up development by allowing components to be designed in parallel with the final product.

Downstream partnerships develop out of the total quality view that satisfying customer needs is the ultimate aim. From this develops the customer problem-solving approach to product supply and the servicisation of manufacture.

Business process re-engineering

Perhaps not a direct by-product of JIT, but certainly a response to the substantial competitive advantage a successful JIT implementation generates, **business process re-engineering** takes the view that progressive improvement, and even JIT once started, is a progressive improvement philosophy, will eventually hit a barrier of diminishing returns.

BPR is a reincarnation of the 1960s' systems thinking philosophy. This assumed that if clear objectives were defined, then a system could be designed to optimally meet those objectives within a given environment. When applied to commercial organisations, a business can in theory be re-engineered to meet any given set of objectives. Usually the objectives are customer-centred; a simple objective might be:

'To generate profit through satisfying customer needs.'

The classical functional divisions, which rarely seem to have much bearing on satisfying customers, would be replaced by a more organic and customer-focused structure in which everyone was concerned with customer service and satisfaction. There is much common ground between BPR and total quality, which is also aimed at customer satisfaction and involves the whole organisation. BPR would also seem to imply the servicisation of manufacture, in that the objective chosen need not be limited merely supplying a product that will meet customer needs.

SUMMARY

Whether JIT has brought about a sea change in operations, or is merely a symptom of a deeper movement, the current climate in manufacturing is leading to a much more customer-centred approach. The various approaches share a considerable degree of commonality, aiming towards lean and responsive organisations establishing strong partnerships on both sides of the supply chain. The human resource within the organisation is also becoming more valued, with the breakdown of the Taylorist principles of the division of labour and hierarchic control. Whether this leads to greater job satisfaction or simply greater stress remains to be seen.

QUESTIONS

Considering your example organisation, what barriers are there to the implementation of the JIT philosophy? How might these be overcome?

FURTHER READING

A starting point for further study of JIT is given by the following books.

Schniederjans, M. J. (1993) *Topics in Just in Time Management*, Allyn & Bacon.

Schonberger, R. J. (1986) *World Class Manufacturing: The Lessons of Simplicity Applied*, Free Press.

The total quality idea is well covered by:
Oakland. J. S. (1993) *Total Quality Management*,
    Butterworth-Heinemann.

7 Inputs 1: Materials and components

INTRODUCTION

All operations involve inputs. If nothing is input, nothing is transformed. In manufacturing, these inputs take the form of raw materials and components and are obvious physical objects. It is often useful to distinguish between materials that are intended to form part of a finished product, and materials that are used during the process, but which do not form part of the finished product. These latter are usually called consumables, since they are consumed in the process; lubricants and cleaning materials are common examples.

In the service sector, physical components are almost always an important input, but they may in some ways be subsidiary to the customer and can usually be thought of as consumables. This depends upon the viewpoint adopted, and particularly the extent of front office–back shop separation. A restaurant meal is quite literally a consumable, but the kitchen is equally clearly a manufacturing process, and even fits the classic job (a restaurant where meals are cooked to order), batch (a self-service cafeteria, where food is cooked in bulk and put on display) or flow (the hamburger restaurant) classification. In general there is no real reason to distinguish between manufacture and service when considering material inputs. The relative scale of expenditure might differ, but the mechanisms of procurement are the same.

INDUSTRY TYPE

The complexity of material input tends to increase through the supply chain. Five stages are usually distinguished, and it is worth looking at each in turn.

Extraction

This is the first stage in any supply chain. Ores must be mined, crude oil extracted, clay and gravel dredged, and so on. Agriculture can also be seen as very similar to extraction, though the inputs are rather more varied. By their very nature, extraction industries are simple in that they are dealing with a single input plus a range of consumables. The input is not received from another source, but is found *in situ*. The main procurement function is concerned not with identifying and negotiating with suppliers, but with identifying possible sites and negotiating access. It is skilled, technical and essentially long-term. Stocks of raw materials do not exist, but reserves do. The land banks owned by speculative house building companies, for instance, conform to this model.

Refining

Most materials need processing after extraction to make them usable. Ores are smelted, timber is sawn or pulped, oil is refined, wheat is milled into flour. These processes are characterised by dedicated plant that is designed to operate more or less continuously. Some processes are genuinely continuous (e.g. oil refining) while others (e.g. some metal extraction processes) are batch-based, but still produce only one product.

These are still essentially simple operations, there are few sources and types of raw material, and while stocks of raw material may be held, they are usually low compared with throughput.

Manufacture

Manufacture represents the conversion of basic materials into usable products. While extraction and refining are usually carried out by a single organisation on a single site, manufacture may be a multistage process, both internally and externally. A cotton harvest is sold to a spinner, who converts the cotton into yarn; this in its turn will be bought by a weaver who will manufacture fabric from the yarn. An upholsterer might buy the fabric (together with many other materials) to manufacture furniture. The supply chain can be quite long, involving many different companies, and becoming increasingly complex. Manufacture generally involves purchasing raw materials and changing their physical form. Metal ingots are melted down and cast into a particular shape, rough castings are purchased and then machined. Materials are purchased from refiners or other manufacturers or through intermediate stockholders, and after processing are sold on to assemblers.

Assembly

In assembly, components are assembled together to form a finished product. It differs from manufacture, in that the principal activity is one of joining together, rather than changing the form of the inputs. Assembly tends to be characterised by massive complexity. The number of different components in an automobile can be measured in the tens of thousands. All need to be sourced and purchased. Frequently the situation is simplified by purchasing assemblies for further assembly. A motor manufacturer buys the fuel injection system from a specialist manufacturer of fuel injection systems; thus the 2,000 components in the fuel injection system become one component for the car assembler.

Distribution

The distribution stage is not always present. In industrial markets, there is frequently direct contact between producer and customer – for example, machine tools might be purchased directly from the manufacturer. Even in consumer markets direct sales occur, as for example the extensive market in mail order sales of personal computers. Distribution is, however, most commonly handled by intermediaries in the retail market. Large chains purchase direct from the manufacturer to sell on to the end user, while smaller companies often buy from wholesalers. Distribution is concerned with moving goods to the customer, but its more important function is to widen choice while reducing unit size.

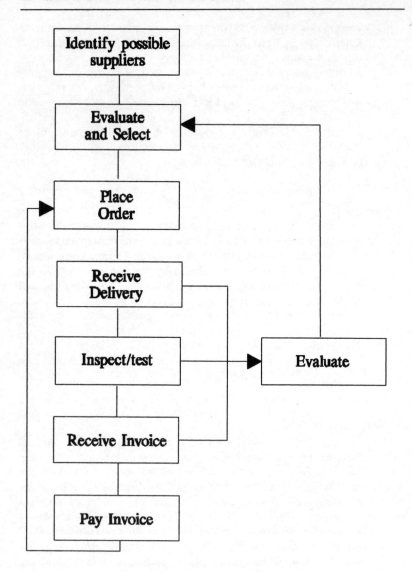

Figure 7.1 Basic material acquisition cycle

THE ACQUISITION PROCESS

At its most complex, the materials acquisition process resembles that shown in Figure 7.1. This is a lengthy and expensive process, and it needs to be carried out for every component and every supplier. Stages are sometimes omitted – many small organisations do not carry out any formal supplier evaluation, for example, but most of the stages are essential. Several ways of simplifying the acquisition process have been developed, but most of these seek to reduce the frequency with which this cycle is carried out. They include:

- *Automation* The use of computer technology and electronic data interchange (EDI), eliminates much of the time and labour involved.

- *Long-term contracts* This involves establishing an overall quantity to be supplied within a given period (frequently a year), and then calling off consignments when needed, or even having regular scheduled deliveries. It simplifies the individual consignment process and can also reduce stocks.

- *Variety reduction* Reducing the number of different materials and components has a major effect upon both the number of transactions and stockholding. This may well damage service in the distributive trades if the customer is seeking wide choice, but there are supermarket chains that trade on a policy of low variety and low cost, passing on the savings that a low-variety policy gives to the customer. In manufacturing variety reduction is a design issue, but the purchase of sub-assemblies rather than individual components reduces both the number of components and the number of suppliers.

- *Supplier reduction* Reducing the number of suppliers dealt with, even without significant variety reduction, confers great administrative savings. There are fewer people to contact if things go wrong, orders, invoices and deliveries can be consolidated, and it is the actual processing of paper which adds cost, not the value of the goods concerned. It is, in part, the obvious saving from supplier reduction that has led to the development of partnership concepts.

PARTNERSHIP

The development of single sourcing and supplier partnerships out of the principles of just in time has been described in Chapter 6. The ultimate aim is for a minimum number of suppliers shipping high-quality components in response to the customer's master production schedule. In retail distribution the same sort of relationship can be established through the use of point of sale data collection and integrated forecasting. Again suppliers are aware of demand almost as soon as their customers. Purchasing is completely bypassed, since the demand is received directly from production. All the transactions become routine, are handled by EDI, and all that is required is a periodic evaluation and reconciliation. The savings are enormous, since most of the steps in Figure 7.1 are eliminated, or take place very rarely. In addition these are taking place in connection with perhaps 50 suppliers instead of 500. On the face of it, this would seem to eliminate the purchasing function, and it does greatly reduce the demand for routine. The function becomes much more strategic, concerned with identifying and evaluating suppliers, evaluating trends, and facilitating negotiations at the user level.

This is a difficult transition to make, and it is not without risk. The traditional approach to suppliers has been adversarial. Suppliers were not to be trusted, since their main motivation was to maximise profit. In addition, suppliers were probably dealing with competitors, so represented a security risk. Given these assumptions, the sensible strategy is to maximise the number of suppliers so that there is always an alternative should one fail, and so that suppliers can be played off against one another to gain the best terms. While this description caricatures the reality, it has a strong influence on buyer attitudes. The buyer is a gatekeeper protecting the organisation against a hostile environment, and is there in part to keep users and suppliers apart. Traditional buying departments see partnership as a threat, both to the organisation and to their own role. Change of attitude takes time, and may fail. It is, of course, always possible that suppliers prove to be unreliable and untrustworthy, and moves towards partnership need to be carefully considered and evaluated.

Several organisations have gone even further and admitted suppliers onto the shop floor, as the following case illustrates.

ABC Company manufactures a range of industrial equipment. It employs a direct workforce of 80, and has an annual turnover of £40m. Apart from the cutting and folding of sheet steel, the main manufacturing operations consist of the assembly of bought-in electrical and hydraulic components, and steel casing to produce finished products. All products are made to order.

The assembly process uses a wide range of fastenings (970 different items), which until recently were purchased from 18 different suppliers using a simple EOQ-based stock control system. Stock was held in a central store and issued to the different production sections against requisitions on a daily basis. In practice, production tended to hold local stocks as well, to avoid the need to go to stores too frequently, and to reduce the perceived risk of stockout. Since no one was formally responsible for these unofficial local stores, they tended to be chaotic and to suffer a high loss rate.

Stockouts were rare, but when they did occur the company would often send someone to a local factor to buy supplies, at considerably increased cost. The potential cost of lost production always far outweighed the cost of this emergency procurement. The frequent processing of orders, together with goods inwards and invoicing, was estimated to be costing £12,000 a year, on a total spend on fastenings of £80,000 a year. It was further estimated that at least 10 per cent of fastenings were lost due to the unofficial local stock points.

The solution adopted was to completely subcontract the fastenings supply system to a specialist fastenings supplier. The supplier provided all fastenings, but also maintained the shop-floor stock. Fastenings no longer went through goods inwards to the main stores. The supplier set up purpose-designed stock points where required on the shop floor, and maintained agreed stock levels. The ABC Company was invoiced on a monthly basis for the fastenings supplied, at a price that included an allowance for the stock service. The total spend on fastenings rose to £83,000 in the first year, but savings in purchasing, stores, accounts and emergency procurement were estimated at £14,000, giving a net saving of about 12 per cent.

SUMMARY

Materials are an essential input into both manufacturing and service operations. Materials can be classified according to whether they form an integral part of the finished product/service or whether they are simply used in the process (consumables); however, this does not greatly affect the issue of acquisition.

The complexity of the material acquisition process depends upon the type of operation involved. Extraction and refining operations are relatively simple, since they deal with a single, or very few, material inputs. Manufacture, assembly and supply operations are characterised by a much more varied material input, and are thus much more complex situations.

A number of approaches to simplifying this complexity have been described, including the use of long-term contracts, the contribution of automation, variety reduction and supplier reduction. Finally, the growing trend towards partnerships has been described.

QUESTIONS

How does your example organisation manage the acquisition of materials and components?

Does it have a formal supplier approval and stock management policy, or is the process more *ad hoc*?

Is there scope for variety reduction?

FURTHER READING

A very thorough treatment of the subject of materials aquisition is provided in:

Bailey, P. and Farmer, D. (1990) *Purchasing Principles and Management,* Pitman.

More recent approaches to the issue are given in:

Lamming, R. (1993) *Beyond Partnership; Strategies for Innovation and Lean Supply,* Prentice Hall.

8 Inputs 2: Labour and plant

INTRODUCTION

In addition to materials to be transformed, operations requires the facilities to carry out the transformation. These are, perhaps, not inputs in the strictest sense, since the objective of the operations system is not to change them, but to utilise them. Any change, and change does happen, tends to be in the form of wear and tear and is therefore undesirable. The choices to be made are broadly between automation and labour, the level of skill of the labour, the reward system used, and in the service sector, the involvement of the customer.

AUTOMATION IN MANUFACTURE

Human labour suffers from a number of drawbacks, when considered in an operations context. People are flexible, able to exercise discretion, able to learn, and, under stress, tend to fail slowly rather than catastrophically. These may sometimes be advantageous, but in a repetitive and predictable situation, they are distinct disadvantages. These failings can be translated as unpredictable, inconsistent, irrational and lacking endurance. Viewed as a component in a production system, the human operator is never perfect, and the only real advantages offered are that labour may be cheaper than automation, and more flexible.

The cost advantages of labour rest partially on the relative cost of wages versus the capital and maintenance costs of machinery. It seems that over the last 50 years, labour costs have inexorably risen, while machine costs have fallen, so the balance has moved steadily towards automation. However, labour costs are revenue costs, and it is relatively easy to get rid of surplus labour, whereas machinery costs are frequently capital costs which must be found prior to production. Once capital costs have been incurred they cannot be recovered, so reasonable confidence in future demand is also necessary to justify automation.

There are some activities that are beyond the capability of machinery, no matter how sophisticated it may be, and these must be carried out by labour, no matter how badly. However, basic human ability has changed little in the past few thousand years, while machine capabilities are advancing rapidly, so again the future would appear to lie with automation. In the service sector there are many activities that could perhaps be automated, but where human interaction is seen as part of the service. It might seem that labour is safe here, but fashions change, and many services (banking, retail distribution, filling stations, for example) have moved from interpersonal interaction to automation or self-service. There is very little evidence of a reverse trend, so even in the service sector the march of automation seems inexorable.

The social and economic consequences of this trend are profound, but they are beyond the scope of this book. Left to its own devices, it would appear that operations management will continue the trend towards automation as it becomes ever more sophisticated and cost effective.

Automation is a term that is not well defined. Most people tend to think of robots, automatic conveyors, machine tools and the like, but automation is also well established in the process industries, such as petrochemical processing where many continuous process are almost entirely controlled by computer.

In manufacturing the development has been fairly clear, and the earliest example of automation is probably the powered conveyor. Thereafter developments took place mainly in the area of metal-cutting. Metal is a stable and predictable material, widely used in manufacture, and many operations basically involve reducing a lump of metal to size. Drilling, turning, grinding all change the shape of the metal by removing excess. The development of automation in metal-cutting followed the following sequence.

- *Manual operation* A skilled operator turning a metal casting on a lathe will adjust the speed of the lathe, and the position and pressure on the cutting tool, to achieve the most economical cutting rate, and to produce a component with finished dimensions that are within specification.

- *Numerical control (NC)* Simple servo-mechanisms are used to drive the lathe and position the cutting tool. These devices were operated by punched paper tape, which was sometimes produced by a device which recorded the movements of an operator, and sometimes punched up directly from drawings. An operator is still required to load the casting, and the cutting tool, into the lathe, to load the paper tape and to supervise the whole process. The saving in total labour is slight, but the skill level required is reduced.

- *Computer numerical control (CNC)* Several machines can be controlled by one computer. The cutting programs are frequently derived from a computer-aided design system, so the whole process is now much more efficient. As with NC, operators are still required, but one operator can supervise several machines.

- *Flexible manufacturing cell (FMC)* Using the increasing sophistication of both computers and servo-mechanisms, the FMC identifies the product from a computer readable code on the workpiece. It then selects appropriate cutting tools from its integral tool store and carries out the operation fully automatically. Operators are required only to mount workpieces on pallets for loading into the machine, and to replenish the tool store as tools wear out.

- *Flexible manufacturing system (FMS)* Here the FMC is coupled with a flexible transfer line, a conveyor system that can route pallets according to the work required and the availability of machining cells. Also included may be automatic inspection devices that can check for dimensional and surface quality of the finished work. Such systems are expensive, and therefore must be fully utilised, but the savings are considerable. A well-run

FMS should operate round the clock (a three-shift system), but only the first shift would be fully staffed. The staff unload pallets of finished work, load up pallets with new work, and ensure that tool stores are replenished. A reduced staff on the second shift simply maintains the flow of work, loading and unloading pallets as necessary, while the third shift is not staffed at all.

Automation has, of course expanded into many other areas. Robots spray paint, weld panels together, assemble circuit boards. Increasingly they are making inroads into fields that are seen as more difficult because of the unreliability of the materials worked with. Wood, for example, is much more unpredictable than metal, but is increasingly being handled automatically. Fabric is particularly difficult for machines to handle, but the problems are being overcome. Automatic cutting, assembly and inspection of clothing will no doubt become a reality, though the traditionally low labour cost of the clothing industry will perhaps delay this.

Dress Well Tailors are a large chain of menswear retailers. While they provide an alterations service, their main aim is to sell off-the-peg men's clothing. To ensure a good customer service without the need for alteration, they carry a wide range of sizes. Jackets come in three lengths and six chest sizes for each length, while trousers come in four lengths and six waist sizes for each length. This means that for each style of jacket or trouser, 24 different sizes are stocked.

The problem is compounded for men's suits. Because of the natural variation in process, the trousers and jacket of a suit must be cut from the same cloth to guarantee a good colour match. This means that a suit must be stocked as a unit, not as a separate pair of jacket and trousers. Since trouser size and jacket size do not necessarily go together, this increases the potential number of sizes for a suit to a maximum of 24 x 24, or 576. Since opposite extremes of jacket and trouser size do not usually go together, this can be reduced to a more realistic 140. Even this is impossible to stock, however, so customers are required to compromise fit on about 50 size combinations.

The development of computer-based fabric manufacture and control has removed this constraint. Fabric is now consistent enough to allow jacket and trousers from different batches of fabric to be combined. Suits no longer need to be stocked as units, and customers can select the best fitting trousers and the best fitting jackets and expect them to look the same.

The effect of this on service is obvious. Suits can now be supplied in any of the 576 theoretical size combinations off the peg. However, the reduction in stockholding is also dramatic, with stocks of matching trousers and jackets being about 40 per cent lower than the stocks of matched suits for the same level of service.

An important consideration in choosing automation is the level of infrastructure support. Automation usually requires a reliable power supply, not always available in some parts of the world. It also requires a labour force prepared to recognise the constraints which automatic plant imposes. Automated equipment tends to be less forgiving and requires a more precise treatment. While labour requirements are reduced, the required level of education and awareness of the labour force is increased. The availability of spares and service is also an important consideration. It may be possible to carry surplus plant capacity when plant is relatively cheap and unsophisticated, but high technology equipment is expensive and must be fully utilised. This means a rapid response is required if problems arise.

AUTOMATION IN SERVICES

In the service sector automation may be used in the back shop in exactly the same way as in manufacturing. Modern banking is completely dependent upon computer processing – it could not function at all in its present form without IT. The majority of this processing power is unseen by the customer and represents an entirely back-shop operation. Automation has also dramatically changed the face of retailing, with point of sale terminals logged on to central computers maintaining completely up-to-date stock records and sales projections, and initiating stock replenishment automatically. Again the direct impact upon the customer is slight; queues are shorter due to bar-code reading and payment is easier using debit and credit cards; but the indirect impact is much greater, with more efficient operations leading to lower costs, and the sophistication of the control system leading to much wider variety and greater reliability in stock.

The effect of automation when it is directly involved in interaction with the customer is rather more dramatic. It is a moot point as to how far automation of a service can go without loss of that service. The two issues that seem to exert the greatest influence on this are:

- the degree to which the customer is prepared to trust machines rather than people;
- the competence of the customer in interfacing with the automatic system.

The issue of trust depends upon the technological sophistication of customers and their perception of risk and cost. For example, people are perfectly happy to trust lifts to automatic operation, and in fact lifts are statistically among the safest forms of transport. Yet people are less likely to accept automatic operation of other forms of transport. Railway transport has been automated in some places, but customer acceptance has proved difficult. Airline operation could probably be fully automated (most flying actually is at present), but few people would be prepared to accept an unmanned airliner. Given that airline disasters have frequently been caused by pilot error, this aversion might seem a little irrational. Automating a service requires a slow conditioning process if the benefits are not immediately obvious.

The competence of the customer is a necessary consideration in designing any service, but if the service is staff-free then it is of paramount importance. Customer incompetence leads to error and delay, not only for the incompetent customer, but for others. The result is poor-quality service. The customers who have been delayed and inconvenienced feel that the service quality has been poor. The customer who caused the problem, however, is doubly dissatisfied, having received a poor service and been made to feel inadequate. Automated services must be designed within customer capabilities. There are still many people who find ATMs intimidating, and who are reluctant to use them just to draw cash, yet the banks, at least in the UK, are actively considering adding facilities such as bill payments, inter-account transfers and the like. The scope for error and confusion is enormous.

The difficulty here is the variation in competence. While some people have trouble drawing cash from an ATM, others are quite happy to run their own bank account directly from a PC, or even, in the USA at the time of writing, to purchase financial services over the Internet. Targeting the service is all-important.

LABOUR

In the previous chapters, the contrast between Taylorism and the newer paradigms of operations have been discussed. The contrast, in labour terms, is not so much one of skill, as of responsibility. Taylorist approaches to operations may employ people with high levels of skill, but severely constrain the field within which that skill can be exercised. This is a particular problem in safety-critical applications, where skilled labour may need to be on stand-by in case of an emergency, but who when things are running normally may have very little of interest to do. There has been some suggestion that the Chernobyl disaster was in part caused by skilled engineers carrying out unauthorised experiments to avoid boredom. If skilled labour is needed then every effort should be made to ensure that the skills are used appropriately. Skilled labour is generally expensive to recruit ready-trained. If trained in-house, then the training costs are high. In either case there is a need to maximise retention. This can be done through motivation; recognising and valuing the skill; or payment, but more usually through both.

Unskilled labour is another matter altogether. It is readily available, and, since recruitment and training costs are low, is not a matter of great concern, at least in economic terms. The just-in-time paradigm suggests that this is an inappropriate view. Labour turnover is waste, since there are termination and recruitment costs regardless of the type of labour. Empowered work-groups are centres of skill and experience regardless of the skill of the individual members, and changes in their composition are damaging. It can be argued that the unskilled worker does not exist in a JIT organisation, and this quest for continuity and commitment has led to such things as the single-status canteen, company uniforms and even the company song. The **learning organisation** is a recent manifestation of this trend, where employees are encouraged to continue training and developing new skills on a continuous basis.

Not all employees like these trends. There are many who are quite happy with Taylorism; who wish to be told what to do and who do not wish to take on any responsibility; who work for money and not for job satisfaction. Such people are still well catered for. Many organisations, particularly in their payment systems, show a marked commitment to the Taylorist paradigm.

PAYMENT SYSTEMS

The whole range of possible payment systems is beyond the scope of this book, so we will consider only the alternatives most commonly adopted in manufacturing. They vary in the extent to which they relate earnings to performance. The theory behind this is that people will work harder if the financial reward justifies it – a perhaps questionable philosophy that is beyond the scope of this book.

- *Hourly paid* Possibly the most common method of payment in manufacturing and service for non-staff positions. Labour is paid an agreed rate per hour for a normal working week, and may be paid at a premium rate for working overtime. The rate of pay is completely independent of output.

- *Hourly paid plus bonus* In this case the basic pay is enhanced by a bonus based upon performance. This may be on an individual basis, but more usually it is group-based. It may be calculated directly from some measured output parameter (i.e. units manufactured, scrap rate, or even attendance), or it may be related to profit. As a motivator this approach has some problems. Profit-sharing in particular may be too remote in time and conception to directly influence work. Many people are occupied in tasks that do not have a direct effect upon profit. The group bonus approach can bring peer pressure to bear, to ensure that everyone contributes, but conversely it can also lead to bitterness and hostility.

- *Direct incentive payments* Here individuals are paid on a sliding scale directly related to their output. Such schemes are

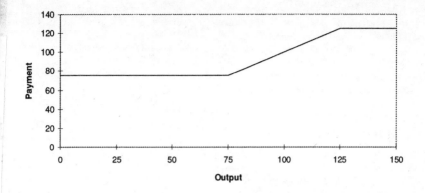

Figure 8.1 An incentive payments system characteristic

usually based upon work measure͘ and guarantee a minimum payment, as illustrated in Figure 8.1. The minimum is intended to allow for a reasonable rate of pay, if difficulties outside the control of the operator prevent the target output being achieved. There is generally a maximum to reduce the temptation to defraud the system by reporting excessively high outputs. Generally operators who consistently perform at below the minimum output will not be retained.

- *Piecework* In a piecework system the operator is paid an agreed amount for each unit of output. In some ways this is the most efficient way of employing labour, though it can represent an almost zero commitment by the employer. Where employees work on company premises there is still usually a minimum output required to ensure that facilities are reasonably well utilised. The ultimate in dissociation between employer and employee is achieved in out- (or home-) working, where the employee provides premises and equipment as well as labour.

Superficially it would appear that dissociation and apparent trust are related to the payments system as shown in Figure 8.2. Kaizen does not fit well with piecework, and an organisation that wishes to empower its labour force and take decision-making down to the

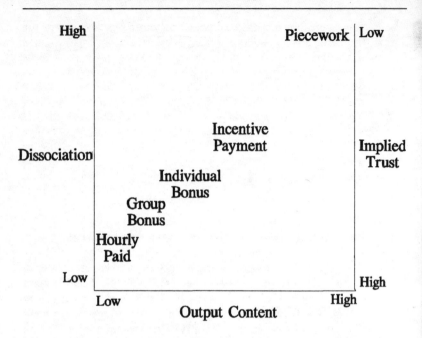

Figure 8.2 Relationship between trust, dissociation and payments system

lowest level should not adopt a payments system which is individual output oriented. This requires close monitoring to function, and close monitoring always implies a lack of trust. An individually based reward system also does not support teamwork. If payment must be related to output then a team-based bonus system is more appropriate, but greater commitment and motivation may be achieved simply by paying a reasonable wage and exercising trust. A JIT approach would argue that monitoring systems, since they do not contribute directly to output, are waste.

CUSTOMER SELECTION AND TRAINING

Employee selection and training is a subject for more detailed treatment within the field of human resource management, rather than operations management, while customer selection is a matter for marketing. In the service sector, however, customer participation has a direct impact upon operations, and customers need to be competent in their role if the operation is to run smoothly. Customer selection is carried out continuously in many subtle ways. Targeted marketing, price, location and physical image are all ways in which inappropriate customers may be deterred. Customer training is less well recognised as an issue. The need for training will depend upon the complexity of the interaction and the frequency of use of the service. Complex processes are difficult to learn, while infrequent processes are not worth the effort of learning, and will in any case be forgotten. Figure 8.3 illustrates this relationship. In practice the difference between customer training and customer instruction is slight. Where customers are expected to learn, through frequent use, instructions are likely to be less prominent. Where a service is used infrequently, or depends heavily upon attracting new customers, instructions must be clear and obvious. These may be written, as pre-printed material issued before the service encounter. An example of this is instructions issued before a hospital in-patient visit, or instructions issued by an equipment service company on the information to have available before calling them. Written instructions in the form of notices are common, but instruction can also be physical, as for example queue fences in banks or barriers at car parks. Devices for preventing wrong actions are always desirable, since it cannot be assumed that customers will read.

In designing customer instruction/training systems, it is important to bear in mind the customer viewpoint. This may seem an obvious point, but unfortunately the designer of instructions usually knows the system well and is all too likely to take too much for granted. The common error of blaming the customer for the service failure, because the customer did not read, or understand, the instructions, is also unacceptable. A service failure is a poor quality service and is therefore always ultimately the fault of the service provider.

SUMMARY

Automation is a continuously developing field, which in both manufacturing and services seems primarily intended to reduce the requirement for labour on grounds of cost and consistency. The

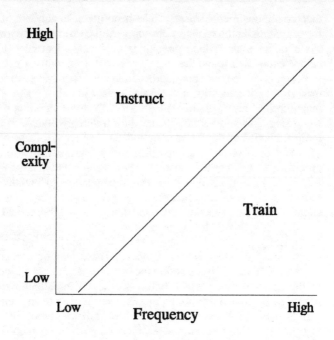

**Figure 8.3 Relationship between complexity, frequency and
training need**

development of automation over the last 40 years has been rapid and
shows no signs of slowing down. The increasing sophistication of
automatic processes has led to greater quality, variety and
availability in all fields in which it has made an impact. The
development of automation in manufacturing has been described and
examples of its impact in both manufacturing and services given.

Labour is not yet obsolete, even in automatic processes, and the
issues surrounding decisions about labour skill have been discussed.
Labour implies payment, and the more common payment systems
have been described. Payment by output systems have been
identified as more appropriate for Taylorist management styles than
for the emerging JIT paradigm.

Finally some consideration has been given to the use of the customer as labour and the implications of this for recruitment and training.

QUESTIONS

How consistent are the management policies and payment systems in your example organisation? Do they preserve an appropriate balance between trust and responsibility?

Consider the clarity and relevance of instruction when you participate in a service encounter as a customer. How effective is it? How much prior knowledge is assumed? How could it be improved?

FURTHER READING

An excellent discussion of the interaction of technology and labour, and the issues associated with the JIT paradigm, is found in:

Storey, J. (ed.) (1994) *New Wave Manufacturing Strategies; Organizational and Human Resource Management Dimensions,* Paul Chapman.

9 Whither operations: The death of management?

INTRODUCTION

In the previous chapters I have tried to outline some of the key elements in the development of the discipline of operations. Operations started in craft workshops, which developed independently throughout history and in all cultures. The principles of batch processing and the division of labour can be seen in the manufacture of poisoned darts by Amazonian Indians just as clearly as in any industrial plant. Evidence of massive flint tool making factories have been found in many parts of Europe. Artisans have always sought to improve not only the quality of their work but also its efficiency. Historically, the formalisation and dissemination of this trend was frustrated by lack of time and lack of a communication infrastructure. Both of these constraints were demolished by the industrial revolution. This led more or less directly to the classical approach (as evidenced by Taylorism and Fordism) of the quest for efficiency through the application of the scientific method. This view was to remain more of less unchallenged for well over 100 years. Indeed, many organisations still proceed on classical lines, but the advent of the 'Japanese way' in the 1970s and 1980s may well have damaged fatally the classical paradigm.

FUTURE TRENDS

Futurology is not an exact science, but if the time scale is long enough, challenges can only be based upon opinion. The extrapolations that follow represent the author's opinion, and while I would suggest it is as good as that of anyone else, it is not necessarily better.

Technology

Quantitative extrapolation would suggest that technology will replace labour within the next 20 years or so. For example, the manufacture of computers and motor vehicles in the 1940s was very labour intensive, while a mere 50 years later manufacturers claim that direct (i.e. manufacturing) labour represents less than 5 per cent of cost.

Early numerical controlled (NC) machine tools recorded and replicated the actions of a skilled craftsman – the modern flexible manufacturing cell will accept data straight from the computer-aided design system and machine the component without human intervention. Automation has developed from simple metal-cutting, to complex cutting, inspection, folding and assembly. It has moved from the relatively simple and predictable world of metal into such fields as electronic assembly, plastics, and the far more difficult area of fabric-cutting and assembly.

Computer-aided design has progressed from what was, in effect, merely a computer-based drawing board, through to complete three-dimensional virtual models of complex products such as airliners. Increasingly, the use of expert systems technology is leading to computers making a major input into design, rather than merely facilitating it.

Taken together, these trends would suggest that the entirely integrated and entirely automatic design and manufacturing process is not far away.

Similar trends can be seem in the service sector, with the development of sophisticated autobanking terminals which allow most transactions to be initiated by the customer. Speculation about virtual shopping using the Internet will certainly become technically possible, and could automate a whole area of retail trade. Automatic checkouts are already in experimental use in supermarkets, so the potential for shopping without any human interaction exists. However, as we have seen, there are very real and unresolved questions about the wholesale automation of services, and it may be that the human interaction will remain a major element. Some supermarket chains are already experimenting with the personal service store-within-a-store concept on a large scale, even moving away from self-service.

Labour

Historically the trend in manufacture has been from the self-managing craftsman to the human component approach of Taylorism. The Japanese Way is seen by some commentators as leading back towards a craft-based system, with delegation of responsibility to the lowest level, empowered self-managing teams and the like. Trends in automation, and the cost reduction aspects of much of TQM, seem mainly designed to eliminate labour altogether. As a result, one scenario might be that those in manufacturing jobs will have a higher level of skill, discretion and responsibility, but there will be few in this position.

Against this trend, many developing countries base their economic development on the availability of low-cost labour, while manufacturers are switching the location of their manufacturing plant to take advantage of this. The economic development brought about by low labour cost manufacture eventually raises the labour cost to the point where some even less developed country becomes more attractive. Eventually an equilibrium between the cost of labour and the cost of automation will be reached.

In the service sector the trend is less obvious. Certainly the balance of employment has moved from manufacturing to service, as shown in Figure 9.1. At the same time, the overall level of employment has increased as populations have risen and more and more women have joined the (paid) workforce.

It seems likely that service operations will prove much more resistant to automation, and will continue to be the major provider of employment. It also seems likely that much of this employment will be low-paid and relatively casual, as for instance in the catering industry. The moves towards competing on quality are likely to bypass a large section of the lower end of the service market. Where

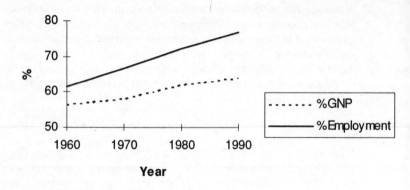

Figure 9.1 Growth in service sector – USA

quality does become an issue of real concern, then this will impose greater demands on service personnel. Skill levels will rise, and, depending upon the predictability of the service, so will the level of responsibility and discretion. In the predictable service, staff will be required to behave consistently, while in the unpredictable service, staff must be empowered to respond to customer expectations.

Quality

For the 'world class' manufacturer, quality of product is already taken for granted. Zero defects are expected, and ISO 9000 guarantees reliability. The arena of competition has moved on to responsiveness and to servicisation. It is the quality of the total support package that the manufacturer provides the customer which matters. Many manufacturers have not yet reached this state. Many never will, as events will overtake them before they realise that the world has moved on. Quality is becoming a market entry criterion.

Similar trends can be seen in the service sector, but the picture is more complicated by the problems of defining quality, and its relationship with value. Once the problem of errors has been dealt with, improving service quality does usually involve greater cost through better staff, better facilities, greater capacity to avoid waiting, etc. As a result there will always be a demand for lower-cost services where quality will be less significant. It is also quite possible that, within limits, quality of service is not particularly important to the consumer.

Supply chain

The pressures of responsiveness and quality have forced manufacturers to establish closer links with suppliers. The servicisation of manufacturing has also forced the link with customers. The result is increasingly close ties between customers and suppliers, a goal that is being pursued from both ends. Only the end customer, in the retail market, has no particular pressure to establish close links with product suppliers. While these links are not necessarily legally binding, in the long term the economic bonds are very strong, with shared engineering and design, shared data and frequently shared working practices. The effect can be seen as similar to vertical integration and may well reduce competition. Industries in all sectors see customer retention as essential, and basically easier than customer acquisition.

Even at the retail end of the chain, organisations are increasingly seeking to bind customers – often, as with discount schemes for regular customers, simply by buying them.

Costs

The impact of automation on costs is debatable, but in the long term it usually leads to a reduction (at least, in the context of the greater flexibility and responsiveness that advanced automation can bring). Of more importance is the effect of automation on cost structures. A heavily automated organisation reduces direct labour costs to the point where they are best treated as overheads. The only truly variable cost is then that of materials and components. Given that this happens throughout the supply chain, and given the close integration which is increasingly developing within the supply chain, the result of this trend is that manufacturing cost are rapidly becoming fixed. Utilisation is still a key issue, but given the flexibility of developing automatic processes, high utilisation will be relatively easy to achieve.

Costs in the service sector seem likely to polarise, with high-quality services being intrinsically more expensive.

THE FUTURE

Taking these influences together, the distinction between manufacturing and service industries is likely to become less significant overall. In the world-class firm, the manufacturing element of manufacturing industries will tend towards a high-quality, fixed cost, largely automatic process. It will, however, be highly responsive, enabling design changes, and even entirely new models, to be introduced on very short timescales. The operations role will become one of systems design and co-ordination. The whole system, integrated back through the supply chain, will depend upon efficient and effective information flow. Meanwhile purchasing and sales roles will become design and co-ordination roles.

At the high-quality end of the service sector (and this would include world-class manufacturers) the operations function would be primarily concerned with ensuring that the service system responds rapidly to customers' requirements. This requires responsiveness and awareness, so the main tasks would be monitoring customer requirements through all means available, but particularly through front line staff, and very active resource management, both for availability and quality. At the low-quality end of the market, where competition on cost will still be a possibility, resource monitoring and management are still vital, though responsiveness will be far less important.

This simple polarised picture will of course not arise, or if it does, it will develop slowly over many years. There will always be customers, both individual and corporate, who do not want to establish partnerships with their suppliers. There are state-run monopolies, which are not subject to the competitive pressures of the open market, where quality and responsiveness will remain subject to the personal inclination of those in the organisation, or the political will of their masters. Voluntary and charitable organisations, while they are subject to competitive pressure in their quest for funds, rarely have to compete for customers. For these organisations, operations management as described in the foregoing, will remain an important discipline.

THE DEATH OF MANAGEMENT

I have implied in the above that the development of automation and supply chain partnerships will substantially reduce the role of operations management in manufacturing. It probably has even more implications for marketing, the role of which, when virtually all sources of competitive advantage have disappeared, seems very doubtful. Advanced manufacturing methods eliminate the possibility of competition on price, on quality, on variety or on responsiveness. This leaves very little apart from service, and if everyone is good at that, then where lies competitive advantage? The majority of the financial services providers in the UK have declared that they will compete on service quality, with several claiming that it will become their distinctive competence. It is difficult to see how the majority of players in any market can claim the same distinctive competence!

Human resource management, presently enjoying a renaissance as new paradigms of operation become fashionable, would also seem to be under threat. The computer-controlled factory, producing computer-designed products, requires little labour, and the general trend of technology is certainly towards the elimination of labour. At more senior levels in the organisation, this trend has not yet manifested itself, but the inevitable, if much delayed, development of expert systems must threaten even the most senior positions.

One question left unresolved by this projection is that of purchasing power. If most manufacturing and service provision is automated, who is going to buy the output of these operations? The social and economic consequences of current trends are significant, yet there is little evidence that they are being seriously addressed. Individual commercial organisations are driven by limited objectives relating to profit and market share. They cannot be expected to take responsibility for the long-term impact of their policies with regard to the development of technology. Some form of accommodation is inevitable, since automatic factories must have purchasers for their output. An orderly progression requires governmental intervention, but there is little evidence of any real will to undertake this.

SUMMARY

Trends in operations management show a certain degree of conflict. On the one hand, increasing empowerment of labour is leading to a collapse of the Taylorist paradigm. On the other hand, the development of technology is eliminating the need for labour. Purely economic pressures would suggest that technology will triumph, and that the reviving status of labour is a temporary aberration.

It is suggested that the unhindered advance of technology will have an even greater effect upon management in general. Many of the functions of management are disappearing, and others are being taken on by increasingly sophisticated automatic systems. This effect is not restricted to operations management alone, but to all management functions. This view might be seen as extreme, and it is probably an exaggeration. For every world-class organisation there are twenty which still seem to be living in the first half of the twentieth century (and even a few for which the industrial revolution has not yet happened). Such organisations have survived, and many will probably continue to do so, but they will be depending upon the ignorance and inertia of their customers, and this is hardly a formula for success.

Appendix: A history of key operations concepts

4000 BC	Egypt	Concepts of planning and control. The idea that a plan must be developed and then monitored to ensure success is central to operations management.
1100 BC	China	Likewise.
600 BC	Chaldean Empire	Production control systems and incentive payments. The first recorded example specific to production.
500 BC	China	Standards of performance and systems of measurement. Principles of specialisation. The precursors of all manufacturing systems up the 1960s.
400 BC	Cyprus	Motion study, material handling and layout. Re-invented in the 19th century as part of the scientific management movement.

AD

15th century	Italy	Part numbers, standardisation of parts, assembly lines, inventory control – all aspects of modern operations management. Recognition of the value of in-

		terchangeable parts. Hand-crafted parts are highly variable, interchangeability depends upon standardisation so that a particular component will fit no matter who made it. An essential prerequisite for any form of mass production.
18th century	Adam Smith	Specialisation in manufacturing.
	Eli Whitney	**Scientific method**. The application of the principles of the scientific method, in particular observation, recording, reproducible and precise measurement to the design and management of manufacturing work.
19th century	James Watt	Standard procedures, standard times. Facilitates planning and control.
	James Mill	Analysis of human motion. Leading into the whole area of work study.
	Charles Babbage	Division of labour, motion and time study.
20th century		
1900s	Frederick Taylor	**Scientific management** – method study, time study, functional structure, need for co-operation between labour and management. Bringing together most of the developments of the previous century into a coherent discipline.
	Frank Gilbreth	Motion study.
	Henry Gantt	Gantt charts, need for training labour.
1910s	F. W. Harris	**Economic lot size.** One of the first applications of mathematical modelling to manufacturing operations.

	Henry Ford	Large-scale development of the assembly line, extreme manifestation of the division of labour.
1910	W. H. Leffingwell	Scientific management in the office. An extension of the work in manufacturing to non-manufacturing activities.
1920s	Dodge and Romig	**Statistical quality control**. Probably the first example of stochastic modelling in operations.
1930s	Mary Follett	Group approach to problem-solving. Not at this time of much relevance to operations, but widely used later in approaches such as kaizen, TQM, JIT.
	P.M.S. Blackett *et al.*	**Operations research**. The integration of existing mathematical models into a unified discipline of mathematical modelling. The most widely used models in operations are inventory, queuing, forecasting, linear programming.
1940s	Norbert Wiener and Claude Shannon	Systems analysis. Again little used in operations management at this time, but a precursor of **business process re-engineering**.
1950s	Armand Feigenbaum	**Total quality control**. The first manifestation of the need to compete on quality. Until the late 1940s manufacturing was operating in a situation characterised by under-capacity, but the stimulus of the 1939–45 war, and the subsequent rebuilding of the German and Japanese industrial bases led to over-capacity and the need for real competition. A broader and more dis-

		cerning market led to quality being one of the areas of competition.
	Japan	**Total quality management**. TQC was mainly design and manufacturing focused. TQM developed out of the Japanese attempts to improve quality and expanded to include all functions and personnel.
	Japan	**Just in time**. Initially arising out of the Japanese motor industry's inability to finance adequate stocks, it became associated with the idea of stockless production in the West, though a broader meaning of continuous improvement through waste reduction is more appropriate.
	Japan	**Kaizen**. An aspect of JIT using small, empowered, workplace teams as the basis for day-to-day management and continuous improvement.
1960s	Douglas McGregor	**Theory X and theory Y**. It can be argued that manufacturing operations management, up to this time, had been predominantly theory X – workers had to be commanded and controlled to produce reasonable output. The more recent group approaches are, of course, ostensibly theory Y.
	Martin Co.	**Zero defects**. Developed initially for high-risk defence manufacture, but widely adopted as a concept throughout manufacturing.
	USA	**Service operations** concepts emerge.
1970s		**Material requirements planning**. High-tech computer-based solution to

the problems of production scheduling. Developed into **manufacturing resources planning**.

Eliyahu Goldratt

Theory of constraints. Also **optimised production technology** and **synchronous manufacture**. The use of throughput rather than utilisation as the driving force behind scheduling.

Simultaneous engineering. Developing, in part, out of **systems analysis**. The simultaneous design of product and process shortens time to market and increases chance of success. Later expanded to include the use of supplier skills in the design process.

1980s

Business process re-engineering. The application of systems analysis to the whole organisation. A reaction against the progressive nature of JIT, TQM, Kaizen. Based on the assumptions that a substantial jump in performance will only be achieved by a radical redesign of the organisation so that its structure matches market needs.

Index